SWU-NAP- 020

UNIFORMS OF RUSSIAN ARMY DURING THE NAPOLEONIC WAR VOL.15

UNDER THE REIGN OF ALEXANDER I
EMPEROR OF RUSSIA BETWEEN 1801 AND 1825
THE GUARDS: HEAVY & LIGHT INFANTRY REGIMENTS

From the Viskovatov's greatest work:
"Historical description of the clothing and
arms of the Russian Army"

English translation by Mark Conrad

SOLDIERSHOP PUBLISHING

AUTHOR

Aleksandr Vasilevich Viskovatov born 22 April (4 May New Style) 1804, died 27 February (11 March) 1858 in St. Petersburg, Russian military historian. He graduated from the 1st Cadet Corps and served in the artillery, the hydrographic depot of the Naval Ministry, and then in the Department of Military Educational Institutions. He mainly studied historical artifacts and the histories of military units. Viskovatov's greatest work was the Historical Description of the Clothing and Arms of the Russian Army.

PUBLISHING'S NOTE

NOTE ABOUT BOOK PRINTING BEFORE 1925

LICENSES COMMONS

ACKNOWLEDGEMENTS

A Special Thanks to NYPL and other institutions for their kindly permission to use some images of his archives, collections or books used in our book.

Title: **UNIFORMS OF RUSSIAN ARMY DURING THE NAPOLEONIC WAR VOL. 15**
The Guards: Heavy and Light Infantry Regiments
By A.V.Viskovatov. Serie edit by Luca S. Cristini. First edition by Soldiershop. January 2018
Cover & Art Design: Luca S. Cristini. Plates re-colorations by Anna Cristini.
ISBN code: 978-88-93273060
Published by Soldiershop publishing, via Padre Davide, 7 - 24050 Zanica (BG) ITALY. www.soldiershop.com

UNIFORMS
OF THE RUSSIAN ARMY
DURING THE NAPOLEONIC
WAR VOL. 15

UNDER THE REIGN OF ALEXANDER I EMPEROR OF
RUSSIA BETWEEN 1801 AND 1825

*

THE GUARDS: HEAVY AND LIGHT INFANTRY
REGIMENTS

The Zar Alexander and an officer of the Guard Regiment Preobraženskij

HISTORICAL DESCRIPTION OF THE CLOTHING AND ARMS
OF THE RUSSIAN ARMY - A.V. VISKOVATOV
(First English translation by Mark Conrad)

Soldiershop is glad to presents the complete collection of the great job made by A.V. Viskovatov dedicated to the uniforms and weapons belonging to the Russian army during the Napoleonic period, until 1825. The time we considered corresponds to the reigns of two Tzars: Paul I, who reigned since 1769 until his murder on the 23rd of March 1801, and his son Aleksandr Pavlovič Romanov, that with the title of Alexander I, sat on the throne until the 1st December 1825.

Our reprint in based on the original 19th century volumes, to be precise the volumes from 7 to 9 are dedicated to the reign of Paul I; this first part is distributed on 7 volumes, having a numbering from 1 to 7. From number 10 to 18 of the original volumes, the second part is dedicated to the Russian troops under Alexander I. These still being worked on and they will be soon ready, distributed on twenty volumes approximately. Our new edition, the first ever published in English, both on paper and digital format, boasts a large number of color plates, many of them unpublished and coloured by our team of expert artists and scholars of uniformology. Each volume is based on 50/70 plates, always accompanied by the original translated text which describes the uniforms, the organization and the armament of the Russian army of the period.

A unique work in its genre, a must have in any respecting collection!

Aleksandr Vasilevich Viskovatov born 22 April (4 May New Style) 1804, died 27 February (11 March) 1858 in St. Petersburg, Russian military historian. He graduated from the 1st Cadet Corps and served in the artillery, the hydrographic depot of the Naval Ministry, and then in the Department of Military Educational Institutions.

He mainly studied historical artifacts and the histories of military units. Viskovatov's greatest work was the Historical Description of the Clothing and Arms of the Russian Army (Vols. 1-30, St. Petersburg, 1841-62; 2nd ed. Vols. 1-34, St. Petersburg - Novosibirsk - Leningrad, 1899-1948). This work is based on a great quantity of archival documents and contains four thousand colored illustrations.

Viskovatov was the author of Chronicles of the Russian Army (Books 1-20, St. Petersburg, 1834-42) and Chronicles of the Russian Imperial Army (Parts 1-7, St. Petersburg, 1852). He collected valuable material on the history of the Russian navy which went into A Short Overview of Russian Naval Campaigns and General Voyages to the End of the XVII Century (St. Petersburg, 1864; 2nd edition Moscow, 1946). Together with A.I. Mikhailovskii-Danilevskii he helped prepare and create the Military Gallery in the Winter Palace.

He wrote the historical military inscriptions for the walls of the Hall of St. George in the Great Palace of the Kremlin. (From the article in the Soviet Military Encyclopedia.)

CONTENTS

*

RUSSIAN ARMY- GUARDS INFANTRY
CHANGES IN THE UNIFORMS AND EQUIPMENT OF GUARDS INFANTRY FROM 1801 TO 1825.

XXXI. Heavy Guards Infantry

XXXII. Light Guards Infantry

Notes.

XXXI. GUARDS HEAVY INFANTRY.
[*Tyazhelaya gvardeiskaya pekhota.*]

9 April 1801 - Lower ranks of the L.-Gds. Preobrazhenskii, Semenovskii, and Izmailovskii Regiments were ordered to cut off their **curls** [*pukli*] and have **queues** [*kosy*] only 4 vershoks [7 inches] long, tying them midway down the collar [1].

21 July 1801 – Generals and field and company-grade officers of the St.-Petersburg Garrison, including the L.-Gds. Preobrazhenskii, Semenovskii, and Izmailovskii Regiments, were given **hats** of a new pattern, completely identical to those introduced on 21 July 1801 to the Leib and Pavlovskii Grenadier Regiments, and already described above [2].

27 October 1801 - Generals and field and company-grade officers, when marching with troops or while on detached duty, were ordered to wear **gray riding trousers** [*reituzy*] instead of white pants [*pantalony*], with brass buttons and leather trim, identical to those established at this time for officers of Army infantry and cavalry [3].

29 December 1802 – Confirmation was given to a new **table of uniforms, accouterments, and weapons** for the three regiments in question, based upon which, as well as upon rules promulgated on 17 March of this year regarding uniforms for Army infantry, combatant and noncombatant ranks of Guards heavy infantry were given the same uniforms as received by Grenadier regiments in 1802. The only differences were in the shape of the headdress, lace sewn onto the coats, and the colors for collars, which in the Preobrazhenskii Regiment remained red as before, in the Semenovskii—blue [*svetlosinii*] with red piping, and in the Izmailovskii—dark green with red piping. in all three regiments the coat's cuffs, skirt lining, and turnbacks were red (Illus. 1873) [4].

Privates or *Grenadiers* had sewn-on lace—two rows on each side of the collar and three on each cuff flap. This was of woolen tape [*sherstyanyi bason*]: in the Preobrazhenskii—red, in the Semenovskii—blue, and in the Izmailovskii—dark green. In each case the tape had yellow stripes and checks. The headdress was a helmet [*kaska*] that was of blackened and lacquered Russia leather [*yuft'*], similar to those which were worn by Army infantry and cavalry during the last ten years of EMPRESS CATHERINE II's reign, but with a higher front plate [*nalobnik*], namely 6-1/2 vershoks [11-3/8 inches]. On the plate was a two-headed eagle of red brass with the monogram of EMPEROR ALEXANDER I on its breast within a shield. The helmet was adorned with a black hair crest [*volosyanyi plyumazh*]; a 2-1/4 vershok [4 inch] wide cloth band behind the crown; a 12-1/2 vershok [4-1/8 inch] long cloth tail [*lopast'*] hanging down the back, with a woolen tassel at the bottom; a black leather lining around the bottom edge; and a likewise black leather chin strap sewn fast to the left side of the helmet but on the right fastened by a black leather button (Illus. 1873 and 1874). The tails were trimmed at the edges and down the middle with gold galloon about 1/4 vershok [3/8 inch] wide. (*Note:*Later this galloon was retained only by non-commissioned officers, and for privates was replaced by woolen tape. But no information has been found as to exactly when this change took place.) The tails and inner side of the front piece were colored according to the regiment: red for the Preobrazhenskii, blue for the Semenovskii, and white for the Izmailovskii. In addition, there were also the following differences:

a) In the First or Leib-Battalion of the Preobrazhenskii Regiment the plate or eagle on the front piece, the edges applied to the rear piece or band along its whole length, and the small grenades on the sides of the band, over the chin strap, were all of gilded brass [*zolochenaya latun'*], and the tail's tassel was white (Illus. 1875a).

b) In the Second Battalion of this regiment the eagle on the front piece and the grenades on the band were gilt [*vyzolochennyi*], while the band was trimmed with red cloth and the same gold galloon on the edges as was sewn onto the tail; the tassel on the tail was dark blue (Illus. 1875b).

c) In the Third Battalion of the regiment the eagle on the front piece and the grenades on the band were brass [*mednyi*] without any gilding; the band was the same as for the Second Battalion; yellow tassel (Illus. 1875c).

d) In the Fourth Battalion—eagle, grenades, and back piece the same as in the Third; red tassel (Illus. 1875d).

e) In the First or Leib-Battalion of the Semenovskii Regiment the eagle on the front piece and the brass and grenades on the band were gilded; white tassel (Illus. 1875e).

f) In the Second Battalion of the regiment—brass eagle and grenades, without gilding; band trimmed with blue cloth and gold galloon at the edges; dark-blue tassel (Illus. 1875f)

g) In the Third Battalion—eagle, grenades, and band the same as in the Second Battalion; red tassel (Illus. 1875g).

h) In the First or Leib-Battalion of the Izmailovskii Regiment—eagle, brass on the band, and grenades all gilded; white tassel (Illus. 1875h).

i) In the Second Battalion of the regiment—eagle and grenades without gilding; band trimmed with white cloth, with gold galloon at the edges; dark-blue tassel (Illus. 1875i).

k) In the Third Battalion—eagle, grenades, and band the same as in the Second Battalion; red tassel (Illus. 1875k).

(*Note*: up to the confirmation of the aforementioned table of 29 December 1802, Guards heavy infantry regiments wore helmets with a two-headed eagle that had in the shield a depiction of St. George the Bearer of Victory instead of a monogram. Even earlier the helmets had a plate covering the entire front piece, of the same form and size as introduced at the beginning of EMPEROR ALEXANDER I's reign for grenadier caps in the Army. But both of these patterns existed for only a short time and were not confirmed. The present description of helmets is in all respects for that pattern introduced by the HIGHEST Confirmed table of 29 December 1802.)

In all these battalions privates had only one shoulder strap on both the tailcoat and the greatcoat, on the left shoulder in the same color as the collar, i.e. red in the Preobrazhenskii Regiment, blue in the Semenovskii, and dark green with red piping in the Izmailovskii. Other uniform items such as pants, boots, neckcloths, forage caps, warm coats, swords (with short-sword blades), sword belts, sword knots, muskets, pouches, knapsacks, and canteens were defined just as for Grenadier regiments.

Non-commissioned officers were uniformed similarly to privates but without shoulder straps; gold galloon (wider than the Army pattern and with a different tracery design) on the collar and cuffs; white plume with yellow and black at the top, of small cock feathers, fixed behind the helmet band on the left side (Illus. 1876) tassel on the helmet's cloth tail in three colors—white, black, and orange, and with the same ring [*trinchik*] as on the sword knot. Like Army non-commissioned officers, they were prescribed gloves with gauntlet cuffs, and canes. In each company four non-commissioned officers had rifled muskets [*vintoval'nyya ruzh'ya*] and the same front pouches [*podsumki*] as in Army Grenadier battalions (Illus. 1876). Four others (including the first sergeant [*fel'dfebel'*] and supply sergeant [*kaptenarmus*] had the same halberds as in Army Fusilier and Musketeer battalions; in the first or *Chef's* battalion of the Preobrazhenskii Regiment with coffee-colored poles, and in the other companies with yellow; in the Semenovskii with black, and in the Izmailovskii with white (Illus. 1877 and 1878). The remaining two non-commissioned officers—an officer candidate and distinguished officer candidate [*podpraporshchik i portupei-praporshchik*] did not have halberds or muskets.

Company drummers had a coat without shoulder straps, closed over the chest with small hooks; with red cloth swallows' wings at the shoulder and sewn-on tape of the same pattern as privates and non-commissioned officers of the Preobrazhenskii Regiment had on collars and cuff flaps; in the Preobrazhenskii Regiment this same tape was used to trim drum belts (Illus. 1879), but in the other two regiments these had no tape. For all three regiments drums were prescribed as for Grenadier regiments, and the color of the drumsticks—the same as the non-commissioned officers' halberd shafts (Illus. 1879).

Fifers had the same uniform clothing as company drummers. In the Preobrazhenskii Regiment there was tape on the drum belts, and none in the other regiments (Illus. 1880).

Battalion and regimental drummers, as well as *musicians*, with the same uniforms as company drummers and fifers, were distinguished from them by gold galloon on the collar and cuffs, and also by having tape along all coat seams, the skirts, and turnbacks, and in seven rows on the sleeves instead of six. As holders of non-commissioned rank, they were authorized the same helmet crests, tassels and tails, sword knots, gloves, and canes as the other non-commissioned officers above, except that the first items, i.e. crests, were of red hair instead of black (Illus. 1881).

Company and field-grade officers and Generals had coats with collars and cuffs of the same colors as for lower ranks, with a gold aiguilette on the right shoulder and gold embroidery on collar and cuff flaps of the same tracery design as established towards the end of EMPEROR PAUL I's reign. Their other uniform items and weapons were the same as for officers in Grenadier and Musketeer regiments, and their spontoon poles were the same color as halberd poles (Illus. 1882, 1883, and 1884).

In regard to uniforms for *noncombatant ranks*, the same regulations were in force as in the Army infantry, i.e. they were prescribed frock coats with collars of the same color as for combatants, and three-cornered hats.

29 June 1803 – *General and field and company-grade officers* were ordered to have *shabracks and pistol carriers [shabraki i chushki]* of the pattern established on this day for Grenadier and Musketeer regiments, and also trimmed with gold galloon. But instead of being dark green, they were red, with silver stars and a colored space between the galloon according to the regiment: green in the Preobrazhenskii, blue in the Semenovskii, and white in the Izmailovskii (Illlus. 1885) [5].

19 October 1803 – Instead of just one, privates were ordered to have **two shoulder straps** [6].

19 October 1803 – For everyday duties and when on maneuvers, combatant lower ranks were ordered to wear cloth **caps** [*shapki*] instead of helmets, of the pattern established on 13 February 1803 for Grenadier regiments but with the addition of a lacquered leather ring or hoop around the top edge, of the width and color of the tape sewn on coats in the Life-Guards Preobrazhenskii Regiment (Illus. 1886). As for Army Grenadiers, the plumes on these caps were black for privates (Illus. 1886); for non-commissioned officers—black with a white top with an orange stripe (Illus. 1886); for company drummers and fifers—red (Illus. 1887); for battalion and regimental drummers and for musicians—red with a white top with an orange stripe (Illus. 1888). For privates tufts, or pompons, were according to the battalion: in the 1st—white outer edge, green center; 2nd—green outer edge, yellow center; 3rd red outer edge, yellow center; 4th, in the Preobrazhenskii Regiment—sky-blue outer edge, white center. For all non-commissioned officers the pompons had two quarters in white and two in white with black and orange [7]. Noncombatant ranks had the same caps but without plumes [8]. At this same time field and company-grade officers began to wear hats with a buttonhole loop of narrow gold galloon instead of being embroidered, with a tall plume as described above regarding uniforms for Grenadier regiments [9].

15 March 1805 – **Helmets**, which had been retained only for ceremonial days and parades, were completely abolished [10].

1 July 1806 – There was the same change in uniforms for regimental and battalion **doctors** as described above in detail for Grenadier regiments [11].

1 October 1806 - The **sheepskin warm coats** [*ovchinnnya fufaiki*] of lower ranks were discontinued [12].

2 December 1806 – Lower ranks were ordered to cut their **hair** short; Generals and field and company-grade officers, however, were in this case allowed to proceed according to their personal inclination [13].

10 March 1807 — Officers' **spontoons** were abolished, and in their place it was ordered that they have **swords** [*shpagi*] when in formation [14].

17 September 1807 — Generals and field and company-grade officers were ordered to wear a gold **epaulette** [*epolet*] on the left shoulder, of the pattern established at this time for Army Generals and field and company-grade officers, but entirely in gold without a cloth field. On the right shoulder there remained, as before, a gold aiguilette (Illus. 1889). In this year Guards officers stopped wearing queues, and continued to powder their hair only for grand parades and appearances at HIGHEST Court [15].

26 September and 19 December 1807 - Lower ranks with **swordbelts** were ordered to wear these not at the waist, but over the right shoulder, under the crossbelt for the pouch, crosswise and with the belts being the same width. In consequence of this the former seventh button at the bottom of the coat's front was abolished. Along with this, the swordbelt as well as the crossbelt were to be stitched along their edges and constructed with a small bend so that the upper edges of both one and the other came closer to the collar. The former **swords** [*shpagi*] with hanger-like blades [*tesachnye klinki*] which had been in use since the time of EMPRESS ANNA IOANNOVNA, were replaced by *swords* [*tesaki*] having a hilt with a large, cupped guard, almost like officers' swords [*shpagi*]. With the new swordbelts, bayonet scabbards were fitted into an opening left in the frog to the right of the sword and are parallel to it, as introduced at this same time for Army infantry (Illus. 1890) [16].

23 December 1807 - Lower ranks were given new **summer and winter pants** according to the patterns confirmed at this time for Grenadier and Musketeer regiments, i.e. the first with spats and the second with leather cuffs provided with seven brass buttons (Illus. 1890). In summertime dress company-grade officers were ordered to wear the same pants as the lower ranks, and in winter—boots below the knee, without cut-outs in back [17].

26 January 1808 - Generals at parades, on designated calendar days [*tabelnye dni*], and at troop formations in general, in peacetime as well as during wartime, were ordered to wear the newly introduced **standard general's coat** [*obshchii generalskii mundir*]. And with the regimental coat when not on duty, they were to have dark-green pants instead of white [18]. (*Note:* The description of the standard general's coat is found below, at the end of the section covering the reign of EMPEROR ALEXANDER I, in the chapter on general-officers' uniforms.)

16 April 1808 – Privates were given **shakos** [*kivera*] of a pattern similar to the caps [*shapki*] introduced in 1804, but lower, being 4 vershoks [7 inches] high. They were trimmed with polished black leather and had sewn-on visors, also of polished black leather. A black leather chinstrap fastened to a brass button on the left side, and there were cloth ear pieces on the sides and a leather flap at the back. Cords were of red and yellow wool, and a plume black hair plume was added, pyramidal in form. In front was a brass two-headed eagle, and above the eagle's crown—a round woolen pompon (Illus. 1891 and 1892). These pompons [repeiki], as before, were white with a green center in first battalions, green with yellow in second battalions, red with yellow in third battalions, and sky blue with white in the Preobrazhenskii Regiment's fourth battalion.. Non-commissioned officers received the same shakos with cords in three colors: white, black, and orange. Their pompons had two quarters of black and orange and two of white. The plume had a white top with a yellow stripe down the middle (Illus. 1893). For company drummers and fifers shakos were as for privates, and for regimental drummers and musicians—as for non-commissioned officers, except with black changed to red [for the plume –M.C.]. Field and company-grade officers were ordered to have the same pattern shako but with cords of silver mixed with black and orange silk, and tassels and slides that were all silver. These shakos were prescribed to have silver pompons with a silver HIGHEST monogram in the center on a field of black and orange toothed stripes; a gilt flat chain on a black chinstrap fastened to both sides of the shako by hooks fixed to small six-pointed gilt stars; and a plume of black cocks' feathers, of the width and height of the plume on officers' hats at this time. Behind, at the center of the top leather trim, was fastened a third gilt six-pointed star with a hook, over which the long shako cords could be slung during marches and while on campaign (Illus. 1894) [19].

14 July 1808 - The round **knapsacks** used by lower ranks since 1802 were exchanged for rectangular ones with two whitened deerskin straps, of the pattern and fitting established at this time for Grenadier and Musketeer regiments. Along with this, it was ordered that when the **greatcoat** was not being worn it was to be placed over the left shoulder, with the ends low on his right side being bound with a whitened deerskin strap. i.e. as practiced in Army regiments (Illus. 1895). Along with the introduction of this new model knapsack and manner of carrying the greatcoat, a new pattern **pouch** was issued, of polished black leather, of the size received at this time in the Army infantry, and with a new pattern badge on which, instead of the previous two-headed eagle, it was ordered to have a six-pointed star in relief, with the inscription: *"For faith and loyalty" ["Za very i vernost']*, and a two-headed eagle in the center. The same badges were issued for non-commissioned officers' front pouches, on which—just as on the other pouches—were kept the previous small grenades in the corners (Illus. 1896) [20].

20 July 1808 - *Officers' gorgets* of a new pattern were confirmed, similar to those introduced this year in the Army infantry but with the addition of a martial armature below the eagle, and for company-grade officers of the Preobrazhenskii and Semenovskii regiments—also the inscription *"1700 Nº19"*, granted by EMPEROR PAUL I in memory of distinction shown at the fortresss of Narva on 19 November 1700 (Illus. 1897) [21].

2 November 1808 - The **pants** authorized on 23 December 1807, with leggings in the winter and spats in the summer, were kept only for combatant lower ranks, while for noncombatants the pants, as well as the boots, were directed to be of the pattern introduced in 1802 [22].

5 November 1808 - Company-grade, when the troops were wearing **knapsacks**, were ordered to also have them, of the same pattern as was established for lower ranks [23].

12 November 1808 – Field and company-grade officers, when not on duty, were allowed to wear dark-green cloth **pants** instead of white ones [24].

27 March 1809 - Instead of one **epaulette**, generals and field and company-grade officers were ordered to wear two. The **aiguilettes** which had been in use were, however, abolished [25].

4 April 1809 - **Noncommissioned officers** were ordered to have **galloon** not on the lower and side edges of the collar, but on the upper and side edges. In this same year the blue shoulder straps of privates in the Semenovskii Regiment and the dark-green shoulder straps of privates in the Izmailovskii Regiment were changed to red [26].

8 April 1809 - There was issued the following order regarding **shoulder slings on muskets**:

1.) The lower bracket on the stock, for the sling, was to be moved higher up to the brass trigger guard.

2.) The button on the sling was to be located two fingers from the upper sling bracket.

3.) A buckle with prong was to be fixed to the middle of the ramrod's brass lower band or tube.

4.) The upper side, i.e. the side paint red, of the sling was to be lacquered so that it would not stain the pouch crossbelt [27].

20 April 1809 - To supplement the directive issued in 1808 concerning new **knapsacks**, the following changes and additions were made:

1.) The **greatcoat** was to be rolled 3-1/2 vershoks [6 1/2 inches] wide and worn over the left shoulder so that the soldier could freely hold his musket behind it.

2.) The lower ends of the greatcoat were to be tied with a strap and buckle 2 vershoks [3-1/2 inches] from the end.

3.) Greatcoat, knapsack, and canteen straps were not to be whitened.

4.) The left knapsack strap was to be worn over the left shoulder on top of the greatcoat.

5.) To hold both knapsack side-straps, there was to be another, third, strap with one end sewn to the left side-strap and the other passed through an iron buckle, with a narrow leather loop. The buckle was to be sewn to the right strap which was bent back under the buckle.

6.) The third, chest, strap was positioned between the first and second top buttons of the greatcoat (Illus. 1898)[28].

30 May 1809 - Noncommissioned officers with muskets and front **pouches** [*podsumki*] had the latter item replaced with pouches [*sumy*] of the same pattern as for privates. Consequently, these men as well as all personnel of non-commissioned officer rank, and also company drummers and fifers, were given shoulder straps on both shoulders [29].

8 June 1809 - The plumage around the sides of **generals' hats** was discontinued and the former pattern of embroidered buttonhole was replaced with a new one made of four thick, twisted cords, of which the two middle ones were intertwined with each other as if in a plait [30].

29 August 1809 – **Halberds** were retained only for first sergeants [*feldfebeli*], while all other non-commissioned officers were given muskets identical to soldiers' [31].

6 December 1809 – Field and company-grade officers were ordered to have *shakos*[*kivera*] with the same flat gilt scales on the chinstraps as established at this time for Army officers, and with the same plume as for privates (Illus. 1899). Generals were not authorized shakos [32]. In this same year canes were abolished, and likewise the hair powder still being used by officers. Both officers and Generals were allowed to wear, over the tailcoat, double-breasted frock coats of dark-green cloth, with the same collar as on the tailcoat, dark-green cuffs, red stamin lining, and gilt buttons [33].

10 February 1810 – Instead of chin straps, lower ranks' **shakos** were given flat brass chinscales. White cords replaced the multi-colored ones, but kept multi-colored tassels and slides for non-commissioned officer. All combatant lower ranks as well as field and company-grade offices were ordered to have a new pattern plume: height—11 vershoks [inches], width at the top—2-1/4 vershoks [inches], at the bottom 1 vershok [1-3/4 inches]. The plume's colors and size were the same as introduced in 1811 into the Army infantry. Officers were also ordered to have entirely silver cords and to shorten the plumes on their hats, so as to be of the shape defined for them in 1802 (Illus. 1899 and 1900) [34].

22 February 1811 – With changes in the composition of the Life-Guards Preobrazhenskii, Semenovskii, and Izmailovskii Regiments, there were also changes in the colors of their shako **pompons** and **sword knots**, as described above for Grenadier regiment, namely:

a) *Pompons*.

1st Battalion, in the 1st Grenadier Company—red for Grenadiers, yellow for Marksmen; in the 1st, 2nd, and 3rd Fusilier Companies—white with a green center.

2nd Battalion, in the 2nd Grenadier Company—red with green at the bottom for Grenadiers, yellow with green at the bottom for Marksmen; in the 4th, 5th and 6th Fusilier Companies—green with a white center.

3rd Battalion, in the 3rd Grenadier Company—red with sky blue at the bottom for Grenadiers, yellow with sky blue at the bottom for Marksmen; in the 7th, 8th and 9th Fusilier Companies—sky blue with a white center.

b) *Sword knots*.

1st battalion, in the 1st Grenadier company—for Grenadiers, red acorns [*derevyashki*], loops [*gaiki*], and bands [*okolyshi*] or *trinchiki*, all yellow for Marksmen; in the Fusilier companies—white acorns with the loops and bands according to the company: in the 1st company - white, in the 2nd - sky blue, and in the 3rd – orange.

2nd battalion, in the 2nd Grenadier company—for Grenadiers, red acorns and green loops and bands; for Marksmen, yellow acorns and green loops and bands; in the Fusilier companies - green acorns with the loops and bands according to the company: in the 4th company - white, in the 5th - sky blue, and in the 6th – orange.

3rd battalion, in the 3rd Grenadier company—for Grenadiers, red acorns and sky blue loops and bands; for Marskmen, yellow acorns and sky blue loops and bands; in the Fusilier companies - sky blue acorns with the loops and bands according to the company: in the 7th company - white, in the 8th - sky blue, and in the 9th – orange.

(*Note:* There were four battalions in the Life-Guards Preobrazhenskii Regiment but since one of them was designated to help form the Life-Guards Lithuania Regiment, there were no instructions given regarding pompon and sword-knot colors for a fourth battalion.)

The lace and fringe of sword knots was left white, as before, with non-commissioned officers having black and orange bands [35].

23 September 1811 – **Forage caps** for combatant lower ranks were ordered to be of the pattern established at this time for Grenadier regiments, but with distinctive band colors: red in the Preobrazhenskii Regiment, blue in the Semenovskii, and white in the Izmailovskii. Piping was as in the Army, in the following colors:

1st Battalion, in the 1st Grenadier Company—red piping at the top for Grenadiers, yellow at the top and around the band for Marksmen (Illus. 1901).

2n Battalion, in the 2nd Grenadier Company—green piping at the top for Grenadiers, green at the top and yellow around the band for Marksmen (Illus. 1901).

3rd Battalion, in the 3rd Grenadier Company—sky-blue piping at the top for Grenadiers, sky blue at the top and yellow around the band for Marksmen (Illus. 1901).

1st Battalion, in the 1st, 2nd, and 3rd Fusilier Companies—white piping at the top and around the band, with the company number on the front of the band (Illus. 1901).

2nd Battalion, in the 4th, 5th, and 6th Fusilier Companies—green piping at the top and around the band, with the company number on the front of the band (Illus. 1901).

3rd Battalion, in the 7th, 8th, and 9th Fusilier Companies—sky-blue piping at the top and around the band, with the company number on the front of the band (Illus. 1901).

Officers were given the same caps but with the addition of a sewn-on visor of black lacquered leather [36].

9 October 1811 – The **halberds** left with first sergeants were withdrawn, and instead they were given soldiers' muskets with bayonets, and consequently they also received cartridge pouches with crossbelts [37].

3 November 1811 – **Gloves** were discontinued for non-commissioned officers, and in their place during winter they were allowed to wear mittens of the same pattern as those used at this time by privates [38].

7 November 1811 – The newly formed *Life-Guards Lithuania Regiment* was ordered to have a coat with a red cloth collar, red cloth cuffs and lapels, and sewn-on buttonhole loops on the collar on cuff flaps. The latter were of tape colored red with yellow for lower ranks, as in the Preobrazhenskii Regiment, and embroidered in gold for officers (Illus. 1902). Shabracks and pistol holders were prescribed to be dark green with two rows of gold galloon with red in between, and with silver stars (Illus. 1902). All other uniform items, accouterments, and arms were prescribed to be as for the three old regiments of Guards infantry, with drumsticks and the handles of entrenching tools to be yellow [39].

1 January 1812 – All combatant ranks of Guards heavy infantry regiments—the Preobrazhenskii, Semenovskii, Izmailovskii, and Lithuania—were ordered to have **shakos** and **collars** of a new style, lower than previously. The first item had a greater spread or widening toward the top and concave sides, and the second was closed in front. Along with these changes, lower ranks were given integral **leggings** [*kragi*] reaching up to the knees, with nine buttons instead of seven, and the previous sewn-on tape on the coats, with a checked design, was replaced with sewn-on buttonhole loops made from yellow woolen tape with red lights or stripes. This tape was also used to trim the coats of musicians, fifers, and drummers. Only in the Semenovskii and Izmailovskii Regiments was the center light of the collar's buttonhole loops the same color as the collar: blue or dark green, respectively. Non-commissioned officers in all regiments did not have two buttonhole loops on each side of the collar, as did privates, but only one (Illus. 1903, 1904, 1905, 1906, and 1907) [40].

With the change in the cut of the collar as described here, there was a change in the gold **embroidery** on officers' coats, consisting of the embroidery being no longer diagonal as before, but straightened to conform to the new upright edges of the collar (Illus. 1908, 1909, 1910, and 1911) [41].

10 February 1812 – **Lower noncombatant ranks** of the four regiments were given the same uniforms as prescribed on 17 December 1811 for these ranks in Grenadier regiments, i.e. gray with red piping, but with the addition of the same buttonhole loops as laid down for combatant lower ranks: one on each side of the collar, and three on the cuff flaps. Shoulder straps were red in the Preobrazhenskii Regiment (Illus. 1912), blue in the Semenovskii (Illus. 1912), white in the Izmailovskii (Illus. 1913), and dark green with red piping in the Lithuania (1913) [42].

13 April 1813 – With the granting to the Leib-Grenadier and Pavlovsk Grenadier Regiments of the rights and privileges of the New or Young Guard and their being titled the *Life-Guards Grenadiers* and *Life-GuardsPavlovsk*, respectively, they were given new uniforms, namely:

Life-Guards Grenadiers – blue [*svetlosinii*] collar with red piping, red lapels or plastron [*otvoroty ili latskany*]; shako and all accouterments and weapons as for the old Guards heavy infantry regiments. Lower ranks kept their white sewn-on tape that they had since 1802, and officers their gold buttonhole loops on the coat collar and cuff flaps (Illus. 1914) [43]. Forage caps were to be as for the L.-Gds. Semenovskii Regiment [44].

Life-Guards Pavlovsk – dark-green collar with red piping, red lapels; officers' shakos the same as in the preceding regiments, and for lower ranks—the headdress established in 1802 but with the addition of flat brass chin scales on the chinstraps; all accouterments and weapons as in the old Guards heavy infantry regiments. Lower ranks were given white thread tape to be sewn onto the coat collar and cuff flaps, while officers received gold buttonhole loops (Illus. 1915) [45]. Forage caps were to be as for the L.-Gds. Izmailovskii Regiment) [46].

In both of these regiments officers' gorgets and shabracks remained as before, i.e. as prescribed for officers of Army Grenadier regiments [47].

In May of 1814 officers of all six regiments of Guards heavy infantry, i.e. Old Guard: Preobrazhenskii, Semenovskii, Izmailovskii, and Lithuania; Young Guard: Grenadiers and Pavlovsk, were ordered to change their previous **riding trousers** [*reituzy*] with leather reinforcements and buttons to ones without leather and buttons, with two wide stripes [*vkladki ili lampasy*] of red cloth along the outer side seams, and on the seams themselves—piping of the same material. In the same year of 1814, on the **cockades** of officers' hats, along the edges of the black tape with orange edging, it was ordered to have another white tape of the same width (of either cotton or silk), which later became silver. In 1815 **drum majors** [*tambur-mazhory*] of the Old Guard, these being the regimental drummers renamed, were ordered to have shako pompons, cords, sword knots, and all lace sewn onto the coat in gold, with the first item having sparkles [*blestki*] and a silver center (Illus. 1916), and the last with small tassels. Instead of sholder straps, gold epaulettes were introduced, of the pattern for generals but with an admixture of red silk (Illlus. 1916 and 1917). These drum majors were given staves with gilded tops in the form of a mace, and with a similar gilt end piece and gold galloon winding around the staff, ending at the lower end in two gold tassels. The galloon on these staves was of the same pattern as on the coat, i.e. with a narrow red stripe down the middle (Illus. 1916 and 1917). Drum majors of the Young Guard were distinguished from the preceding only in gaving their shako cords, epaulettes, sword knots, sewn-on tape, and small tassels on the coat, as well as the galloon and tassels on the staff, all in silver instead of gold (Illus. 1917) [48].

11 February 1815 – Officers of the L.-Gds. Grenadier and L.-Gds. Pavlovsk Regiments were ordered to have the same **gorgets** as the L.-Gds. Izmailovskii and Lithuania, while **shabracks** and **pistol holders** were to be dark green with gold galloon, silver stars, and an insert between the galloon—blue [*svetlosinii*] for the L.-Gds. Grenadiers Regiment and white for the Pavlovsk (Illus. 1918) [49].

24 January 1816 - In all Guards heavy infantry regiments the **scabbards** for short swords [*tesaki*] and bayonets, and subsequently those for officers' rapiers [*shpagi*], were ordered to be black and lacquered [50].

8 May 1817 – In order to make the **greatcoats** of the L.-Gds. Preobrazhenskii, Semenovskii, and Izmailovskii Regiments, in the 1st Guards Infantry Division, different from those of the L.-Gds. Lithuania (renamed the L.-Gds. Moscow on 12 October 1825), Grenadiers, and Pavlovsk, in the 2nd Guards Infantry Division, the first three were ordered to have greatcoat collars the same as before without any change, while the last three were to have sewn-on buttonhole loops or patches [*petlitsy ili klapany*] of red cloth 1-1/2 vershok [2-5/8 inches] long and 1/2 vershok [7/8 inch] wide, with the same buttons on these patches as were on the tailcoat (Illus. 1919). This pattern was for officers as well as lower ranks [51].

12 May 1817 – All combatant ranks in the L.-Gds. Preobrazhenskii, Semenovskii, and Izmailovskii Regiments were ordered to have **coats** with red cloth lapels, cuffs, and cuff flaps, and white cloth piping on the lapels, cuffs, flaps, and skirt turnbacks (Illus. 1920, 1921, 1922, 1923, 1924). Piping on the collar was left red as before, and after this all Guards heavy-infantry regiments were in coats with lapels that in winter were ordered to be closed , i.e. buttoned one over the other, except for parades and ceremonial days, and to be open all the rest of the time [52].

13 May 1817 - In order to relieve the soldier while on campaign and to protect his accouterments, it was laid down that during such times they were always to be in greatcoats and their shako, plume, pouch, and uniform with leggings were to have **covers** [*chekhly*] of raven's-duck or Flemish linen painted with black oil paint in the manner of oilcloth, in all respects according to the instructions laid out in detail above in the description of uniforms for Grenadier regiments [53].

8 August 1817 - The size of the **forage cap** was laid down as described above in detail for Grenadier regiments [54].

26 September 1817 – Confirmation was given to a description of **accouterments** and instructions for the manner of wearing them in the Guards heavy infantry, identical to those issued at this time for Grenadier regiments, with only the following differences:

a) All metallic items prescribed to be made of iron in Grenadier regiments were left in the Guards as before, of red brass [*krasnaya med'*, or copper] (Illus. 1925, 1926, and 1927). In only the L.-Gds. Pavlovsk. Regiment were the shako's badge, small grenades, and chin scales left of yellow brass (Illus. 1927) [55].

b) On the shako, instead of an oblong badge with star and crown, the two-headed eagle was left as before (Illus. 1925 and 1926) [56].

c) On the pouch cover, instead of a grenade with three flames, there were kept a round badge of the previous pattern in the center, and small single-flame grenades in the corners [57].

d) The buckle fastening the knapsack's chest strap was prescribed to be of red brass instead of iron [58].

e) All straps for the knapsack and canteen were prescribed not to have stitching along the sides [59].

8 December 1817 – It was ordered that the **leather cuffs on cloth pants** were to have spat-like projections [*kozyr'ki*] of a pattern similar to the spats on summer pants [60].

2 March 1818 – The newly established *L.-Gds. Lithuania Regiment* in Warsaw was prescribed to have the same uniform as the old regiment of that name, but with yellow collar, lapels, and cuffs; white buttons and shako fittings; cloth pants with integral spats instead of leather leggings, after the pattern used in the Grenadier, Carbineer, Infantry, and Jäger regiments of the Separate Lithuanian Corps; instead of an image of St. George the Bearer of Victory within shako badges and the arms on officers' gorgets—an image of the Lithuanian coat-of-arms, i.e. a galloping horseman; silver buttonhole loops on officers' coats; yellow shabracks and pistol holders with silver galloon and dark-green trim (Illus. 1928, 1929, 1930, 1931, and 1932) [61].

23 August 1818 – The length and width of **shoulder straps** on tailcoats and greatcoats was defined, identical to that laid down at this time for Grenadiers and other Army infantry regiments [62], and it was confirmed that musicians' and drummers' coats would have shoulder wings or swallows' nests [*plechevye klapany ili kryl'tsa*] of the the same color as the shoulder strap—red (Illus. 1933, 1934, and 1935). In Old Guard regiments, the sewn-on tape on these coats was yellow with one red and four orange stripes (Illus. 1933 and 1934), while in the Young Guard—Grenadiers and Pavlovsk—it was white with one red stripe (Illus. 1935) [63].

25 January 1819 – **Drumsticks** and the **handles of entrenching tools** were ordered to be be straw-colored in the Preobrazhenskii, Moscow, and Lithuania regiments; black in the Semenovskii and Grenadiers; and white in the Izmailovskii and Pavlovsk [64].

4 April 1819 - The **spats** on the leggings in use since 1817 were removed [65].

10 April 1819 - The *hornists* [*gornisty*] and *signalers* [*signalisty*] newly placed on the establishment of Guards heavy infantry regiments were authorized the same uniform as for drummers, and the **signal horns** [*signalnye rozhki*] were to be of yellow brass, with white straps, and painted inside with red paint, with a gold wreath around the edge (Illus. 1936) [66].

20 September 1820 – Field and company-grade officers of Guards heavy infantry regiments were given a new pattern *gorget*, identical to that established at this time for Grenadier and other regiments of Army infantry, but with the addition of a stand of arms (Illus. 1937). In this same year there was a change in the uniforms of musicians, fifers, signalers, and drummers, consisting of the sewn-on chevrons on their coats beginning to be placed closer together, almost touching one another, and on the swallows' nests the tape was no longer perpendicular as before, but at a diagonal toward the lower edge. Also, all four sides of the collar began to be trimmed with this tape (Illus. 1938) [67].

26 November 1823 - All **musicians** of the named regiments, even though they might not hold non-commissioned officer ranks, were ordered to have: gold galloon on the coat; plumes on the shakos with noncommissioned officers's tops and non-commissioned officers' pompons. This did not apply to hornists, fifers, or drummers who did not hold non-commissioned officer rank [68].

16 January 1824 – The following changes were ordered in the uniforms and accouterments of combatant lower ranks:

1) **Coattails**, which up to this time had one covering the other, were to be cut so that their inner edges came together, and sewn together where they touched (Illus. 1939).

2.) To the decorative end [*trinchik*] of the **shako cords**, which was to be level with the right shoulder, there was to be added a special loop of white cord attached to the button on the right shoulder strap, so that the shako cords stayed in place when the soldier moved about (Illus. 1939).

3.) The **cartridge pouch** was to be worn so that when the soldier bent his elbow, the distance between it and a line with the top edge of the pouch was equal to 3 vershoks [5 1/4 inches].

4.) The **knapsack chest strap** was to be fitted so that it passed between the third and fourth buttons of the coat, as counted from the bottom (Illus. 1939).

5.) On the **musket sling**, opposite the cocking piece, there was to be a band of the same kind of leather as the sling, for stowing the firing cover [*ognivnyi chekhol*] when it needed to be removed (Illus. 1939) [69].

29 March 1825 - For combatant lower ranks, for faultless service, there were established **stripes** [*nashivki*] to be sewn on the left sleeve: for 10 years service - one, for 15 years - two, for 20 years - three; one over the other, all of yellow tape [70].

In May of 1825 – Officers of the **L.-Gds. Pavlovsk Regiment**, instead of their shakos with plumes, were ordered to wear **headdresses** [*shapki*] of the pattern prescribed for lower ranks but with gilded front plates, chinscales, and small grenades. The body was to be trimmed with silver galloon, and it was to have a silver tassel with a mixture of black and orange silk in its center. In front was a silver HIGHEST monogram under a crown, of the same appearance as prescribed for officers' shako pompons (Illus. 1939a) [71].

XXXII. GUARDS LIGHT INFANTRY.
[*Legkaya gvardeiskaya pekhota.*]

9 April 1801 - Lower ranks of the L.-Gds. Jäger Battalion were ordered to cut off their **curls** and have **queues** only 4 vershoks [7 inches] long, tying them midway down the collar [72].

18 May 1801 – The L.-Gds. Jäger Battalion, instead of white cloth **pants**, was ordered to issue green, but in summer—white linen pants, reaching to below the calf to the instep [73].

21 June 1801 - Generals and field and company-grade officers of the L.-Gds. Jäger Battalion were given **hats** of a new pattern, completely identical to those introduced on 21 June 1801 [sic, 24 June in the chapter for Grenadiers – M.C.] to the Leib and Pavlovskii Grenadier Regiments, and already described above [74].

27 October 1801 - Generals and field and company-grade officers, when marching with troops or while on detached duty, were ordered to wear **gray riding trousers** [*reituzy*] instead of white pants [*pantalony*], with brass buttons and leather trim, identical to those established at this time for officers of Army infantry and cavalry [75].

16 September 1802 – Lower ranks of the L.-Gds. Jäger Regiment were ordered to have **round hats** [*kruglyya shlyapy*] of the pattern established at this time for Army jägers, but for privates with tape around the top, this tape being the same as on the coat's collar and cuffs (Illus. 1940). For non-commissioned officers this was replaced by gold galloon (Illus. 1940). The small tassels on these hats were orange with a green center (Illus. 1940 and 1941) [76].

29 December 1802 - Confirmation was given to a new **table of uniforms, accouterments, and weapons** for the L.-Gd. Jäger Battalion. Based on this table as well as upon rules promulgated on 17 March of this year for Army infantry, combatant and noncombatant ranks in the battalion were given the same uniforms Army Jäger regiments had at the close of 1802, but with slit cuffs without flaps. These cuffs were orange, as were the collar and piping on skirt turnbacks and pants, and furthermore had tape—the same as in the Preobrazhenskii Regiment-sewn onto the collar and cuffs (Illus. 1940). In regard to other uniform clothing items, as well as arms and accouterments, private jägers, non-commissioned officers, company and battalion drummers, waldhornists, and officers all were prescribed the same as for these ranks in Army Jäger regiments, except that the last—the officers—wore a gold aiguilette on the right shoulder in the manner of the rest of the Guards (Illus. 1940, 1941, 1942, 1943, and 1944) [77].

29 June 1803 Generals and field and company-grade officers were ordered to have **shabracks** and **pistol carriers** of the pattern established on this day for Army Jäger regiments: light green with gold galloon and orange trim and piping (the same color as the collar). The shabrack also had the same silver stars as in Guards heavy infantry regiments (1945) [78].

5 January 1804 – **Drum slings and hoops** in the L.-Gds. Jäger Battalion were ordered to be black [79].

7 August 1804 – **Musket and rifle slings** [*ruzeinye i shtutsernye remni*] in the L.-Gds. Jäger Battalion, instead of being red, were ordered to be black. In this same year Generals and field and company-grade officers were given **hats** with a buttonhole loop of narrow gold galloon, and with a tall green plume, as high as before (Illus. 1946) [80].

19 October 1804 – Instead of round hats, lower combatant ranks in the L.-Gds. Jäger Battalion were given **cloth caps** [*shapki*] of the pattern received at this time by lower ranks in Guards heavy infantry regiments, but without a plume, yet with the same two small tufts as were on the hats, i.e. orange outside, and a green center (Illus. 1947 and 1948) [81].

1 October 1806 - The **sheepskin warm coats** [*ovchinnnya fufaiki*] of lower ranks were withdrawn [82].

18 October 1806 – The previous cartridge pouches [*patrontashi*] of the Jägers were replaced with **front pouches** [*podsumki*] measuring 7-1/2 vershoks [13-1/8 inches] long and 3 vershoks [5-1/4 inches]wide (Illus. 1949) [83].

2 December 1806 - Lower ranks were ordered to cut their **hair** short; Generals and field and company-grade officers, however, were in this case allowed to proceed according to their personal inclination [84].

17 September 1807 - Generals and field and company-grade officers of the L.-Gds. Jäger Regiment were ordered to wear a gold **epaulette** on the left shoulder, of the pattern established at this time for Army Generals and field and company-grade officers of Guards heavy infantry (Illus. 1950) [85]. In this year Guards Jäger officers stopped wearing **queues**, and continued to powder their hair only for grand parades and appearances at HIGHEST Court [86].

26 September 1807 – Instead of front pouches, lower ranks of the L.-Gds Jäger Regiment were ordered to have **pouches** [*sumy*] of the same pattern as those used by Guards heavy infantry, but without a badge on the cover, and on a black crossbelt [87].

7 November 1807 – In the L.-Gds. Jäger Regiment the light-green color of coats and pants, as well as of shabracks and pistol carriers, was changed to **dark green** [88].

19 December 1807 – Lower ranks of the regiment were ordered to wear the **sword belt** not around the waist, but over the right shoulder, in all ways conforming to what was established at this time for Guards heavy infantry. In consequence of this the former seventh button at the bottom of the coat's front opening was abolished, and two shoulder straps of orange cloth were to be worn on the tailcoat as well as the greatcoat (Illus. 1951) [89].

23 December 1807 - Lower ranks were given new **summer and winter pants** according to the patterns confirmed at this time for Grenadier and Musketeer regiments, i.e. the first with spats and the second with leather reinforcements or cuffs provided with seven brass buttons (Illus. 1951, 1952, and 1953) [90].

26 January 1808 - Generals at parades, on designated calendar days [*tabelnye dni*], and at troop formations in general, in peacetime as well as during wartime, were ordered to wear the newly introduced **standard general's coat** [*obshchii generalskii mundir*]. And with the regimental coat they were to have dark-green pants instead of white when not on duty [91].

16 April 1808 – In the L.-Gds. Jäger Regiment lower combatant ranks and officers were given **shakos** [*kivera*] of the pattern confirmed for Guards heavy infantry, except without plumes. Also about this same time they were ordered to have dark-green cloth flaps with orange piping on the tailcoat's cuffs, with three buttons and buttonhole loops on each, these loops being the same as on the collar. The green plumes of officers were replaced by black ones (Illus. 1951, 1952, and 1953) [92].

On this same day there was a HIGHEST Order whereby the *Battalion of Finnish Guards* or **L.-Gd. Finland Battalion**, renamed from the battalion of IMPERIAL Militia and attached to the Guards light infantry, were to have shako plates and buttonhole loops on the coat of the same patterns as used in the L.-Gds. Jäger Regiment. The uniform of the L.-Gds. Finland Battalion, consisting of one Grenadier and four Jäger companies, was thereupon distinguished from that of the Guards Jägers by being dark green with red piping, collar, lapels, and cuffs, and the red color of their shoulder straps and the red piping on cuff flaps, turnbacks, and pants. In addition, the skirts of officers' coats did not have horizontal pocket flaps, while Grenadiers (not authorized in the L.-Gds. Jäger regiment) had thick hair plumes. (*Note:* There was also an Artillery half-company with this battalion, covered below in the section for uniforms of Guards Foot Artillery.) The battalion's accouterments and arms were also the same as for Jägers, with the distinction that all lower combatant ranks—except privates in Jäger companies, who had bayonets—wore short swords in black leather scabbards. The swords had hilts without a cup-like guard, a black leather grip wound with brass (Illus. 1954, 1955, and 1956). Officers wore similar half-sabers (Illus. 1957) [93], and their shabracks and pistol carriers—as in the L.-Gds. Jäger Regiment—were dark green with two rows of gold galloon and silver stars, but with dark-green inserts instead of orange, and with red piping (Illus. 1958). The was also a difference in the knapsacks of the L.-Gds. Jäger Regiment and the L.-Gds. Finland Battalion: in the former they were round and worn carried by one strap over one shoulder, while in the latter they were rectangular and carried by two straps over both shoulders [94].

25 June 1808 – All lower combatant ranks of the L.-Gds. Jäger Regiment were ordered to have muskets with triangular cross-section **bayonets** instead of the former flat ones. These were to always be fixed when in formation, and thereafter the twelve rifles [*shtutsera*] with daggers [*kortiki*] in each company were no longer used. With this change, all private Jägers were given bayonet scabbards for their sword belts, while other lower combatant ranks had swords [*shpagi*] with short-sword blades, like those in the Guards heavy infantry (Illus. 1959) [95].

14 July 1808 – Instead of their round **knapsacks** worn over one shoulder, lower ranks of the L.-Gds. Jäger Regiment were given rectangular ones with two black straps, of a pattern and fitting identical to that introduced at this time in the Guards heavy infantry, and already in use in the L.-Gds. Finland Battalion. In regard to the wearing of these knapsacks and **greatcoats**, when the latter was not actually put on by personnel it was ordered that it be carried in accordance with the directives issued to the L.-Gds. Preobrazhenskii, Semenovskii, and Izmailovskii Regiments (Illus. 1959) [96].

2 November 1808 - The **winter pants** with leggings and the **summer pants** with spats, authorized on 23 December 1807, were kept only for combatant lower ranks, while for noncombatants pants, as well as boots, were directed to be of the pattern introduced in 1802 [97].

5 November 1808 - Company-grade officers, when the troops were wearing **knapsacks**, were ordered to also have them, in all details of the same pattern in was established for lower ranks [98].

21 January 1809 – Confirmation was given to a table of uniforms, accouterments, and arms for the **L.-Gds. Finland Battalion**, based upon which it kept all the same uniform clothing and weapons as indicated above, with the addition of only a paragraph for *noncombatant lower ranks*, who by this table were prescribed to have: dark-green single-breasted frock coats with red piping on the collar and cuffs, with brass buttons; dark-green pants without piping, worn in boots as prescribed in 1802 for all lower ranks; and the same shako as for combatant ranks but without cords, with a a small single-flame grenade instead of an eagle (Illus. 1960). Personnel holding non-commissioned officer rank had gold galloon on the collar and cuffs, a non-commissioned officer pompon on the shako, gloves, and a cane (Illus. 1960) [99].

4 April 1809 - **Noncommissioned officers** were ordered to have **galloon** not on the lower and side edges of the collar, but on the upper and side edges [100].

8 and 20 April 1809 – The changes introduced at this time for Guards heavy infantry regarding **musket slings**, the rolling and carrying of the **greatcoat**, and the addition of a third, chest, strap to the **knapsack**, were applied with equal force to Guards light infantry (Illus. 1961) [101].

24 May 1809 – Field and company-grade officers of the L.-Gds. Jäger Regiment and Finland Battalion were given **gorgets** of the same pattern as used at this time by field and company-grade officers of the L.-Gds. Izmailovskii Regiment [102].

8 June 1809 - **Hat plumage** for general officers was removed and the previous pattern of embroidered buttonhole was replaced with a new one consisting of four thick bullion cords of which the middle two were interwoven together in the form of a plait [103].

6 December 1809 - Field and company-grade officers were ordered to have *shakos* [*kivera*] with flat gild chinscales, as established at this time for officers of Guards heavy infantry. In the Grenadier Company of the L.-Gds. Finland Battalion the shako additionally had a black hair plume while the battalion's remaining companies, as well as the entire L.-Gds. Jäger Regiment, had no plumes (Illus. 1962). Generals were not authorized shakos [104]. In this same year canes were abolished, as well as the hair powder still being used by officers. Officers and generals were allowed to wear double-breasted frock coats of dark-green cloth, with the same collar as on the tailcoat except without buttonhole loops, dark-green cuffs, dark-green stamin lining, and gilt buttons [105].

10 February 1810 – In the L.-Gds. Jäger Regiment and L.-Gds. Finland Battalion it was ordered that the **shakos** of lower ranks replace the chinstrap with flat brass chinscales, and have white cords instead of multicolored, although non-commissioned officers would have multicolored tassels and slides. The Grenadier Company of the L.-Gds. Finland Regiment was also ordered to have a new pattern plume: 11 vershoks [19-1/4 inches] high, 2-1/4 vershoks [4 inches] wide at the top and 1 vershok [1-3/4 inches] wide at the bottom, of the same size and colors as those introduced at this time in the Guards heavy infantry (Illus. 1963). Officers were furthermore ordered to have all-silver shako cords and to shorten the hat plume to conform to the pattern granted in 1802 [106].

5 September 1810 – Instead of orange collars and cuffs, the L.-Gds. Jäger Regiment was ordered to have these in **dark green** with only the piping being orange (Illus. 1963). This piping was also given to officers' shabracks and pistol carriers, and the orange light or insert that showed between the two rows of gold galloon was replaced by dark green (Illus. 1964) [107].

22 February 1811 – With the L.-Gds. Jäger Regiment being brought to a three-battalion configuration, each of one Grenadier and three Jäger companies, it was ordered to have the same **pompon** and **sword-knot** colors as described in detail above for heavy Guards infantry: for Grenadiers—as for Grenadiers, for Jäger non-commissioned officers—as for fusilier non-commissioned officers. Officers and lower ranks of Grenadier platoons, as well as the regimental drummer, were directed to wear shakos with the plumes prescribed at this time for Guards heavy infantry and the L.-Gds. Finland Battalion (Illus. 1965, 1966, and 1967) [108].

23 September 1811 – Lower ranks in the L.-Gds. Jäger Regiment were ordered to have a new pattern **forage cap**, the same as received at this time by regiments of Guards heavy infantry, but with an orange band to match the piping color. Company distinctions were found in the piping, which was prescribed to be:

1st Battalion, in the 1st Grenadier Company: red on top for Grenadiers; yellow on top and around the band for Marksmen (Illus. 1968).

2nd Battalion, in the 2nd Grenadier Company: green on top for Grenadiers; green on top and yellow around the band for Marksmen (Illus. 1968).

3rd Battalion, in the 3rd Grenadier Company: sky blue on top for Grenadiers; sky blue on top and yellow around the band for Marksmen (Illus. 1968).

1st Battalion, in the 1st, 2nd, and 3rd Jäger Companies: white on top and around the band, with the company number on the front of the band. (Illus. 1968).

2nd Battalion, in the 4th, 5th, and 6th Jäger Companies: green on top and around the band, with the company number on the front of the band. (Illus. 1968).

3rd Battalion, in the 7th, 8th, and 9th Jäger Companies: sky blue on top and around the band, with the company number on the front of the band. (Illus. 1968).

Officers were given the same forage caps except without numbers and with the addition of a sewn-on visor of black lacquered leather [109].

19 October and 11 November 1811 – With the L.-Gds. Finland Battalion being renamed the **L.-Gds. Finland Regiment** and brought to a strength of three battalions, each of one Grenadier and three Jäger companies, it was prescribed the same colors for sword knots, shako pompons, and forage caps was were in the L.-Gds. Jäger Regiment, except that the forage-cap bands were dark green (Illus. 1968) [110]. From this same time the half-sabers previously used by lower ranks and officers werer replaced with standard infantry short swords [*tesaki*] and officers swords [*shpagi*] [111].

3 November 1811 – Gloves were withdrawn from non-commissioned officers, and they were allowed in winter to wear **mittens** identical to those used at the time by privates [112].

1 January 1812 – All combatant ranks of both regiments of Guards light infantry were ordered to have pattern **shakos** [*kivera*] and collars, lower than before. The first had a noticeable spread or widening toward the top and indented sides, and the second was closed in front. Along with this change, lower ranks were given knee-length leggings with nine buttons instead of seven, and the previous sewn-on tape for coats with a checked tracery pattern was replaced by sewn-on buttonhole loops of yellow woolen tape, in the L.-Gds. Jäger Regiment with red rays or stripes [*reiki ili poloski*], and in the L.-Gds. Finland Regiment with red and—in the center—black, stripes. This tape was also used to trim the coats of musicians, fifers, and drummers (Illus. 1969, 1970, 1971, and 1972) [113]. With the change in the cut of the collar described here, there was also a change in the embroidered gold buttonhole loops on officers' coat collars, consisting of the loops receiving a new straight orientation and no longer being slanted as previously, similar to the change described above for the gold buttonhole loops on officers' collars in the L.-Gds. Lithuania Regiment (Illus. 1969, 1970, and 1972) [114]. [*Note: This is not exactly what was written in the referenced paragraph, since the buttonhole loops of the Lithuania Regiment were not, in fact, specifically mentioned – M.C.*]

10 February 1812 – **Lower noncombatant ranks** of the L.-Gds. Jäger and Finland Regiments were given the same uniforms as prescribed on this date for noncombatant personnel of Guards heavy infantry, but with dark-green piping instead of read, and with shoulder straps according to the regiment: in the Jäger Regiment—orange, and in the Finland Regiment—dark green with red piping (Illus. 1973) [115].

20 May 1814 – For campaigns, officers of both regiments were ordered to change their previous **riding trousers** [*reituzy*] with leather reinforcements and buttons to ones without leather and buttons, with two wide stripes [*vkladki ili lampasy*] of dark-green cloth along the outer side seams, and on the seams themselves—piping of red cloth [116].. In the same year of 1814, officers were ordered to have a cockade on the hat with white tape around it, which later was changed to silver, and from 1815 **drum majors** [*tambur-mazhory*], these being the regimental drummers renamed, were given the same uniforms as received at this time by drum majors in the Guards heavy infantry regiments (Preobrazhenskii, Semenovskii, Izmailovskii, and Lithuania), i.e. the Old Guard [117].

24 January 1816 – In the light Guards infantry the **scabbards** for short swords [*tesaki*], and subsequently those for officers' rapiers [*shpagi*], were ordered to be black and lacquered [118].

3 February 1816- It was ordered that **officers' tailcoats** in the L.-Gds. Jäger Regiment have skirttails without horizontal pocket flaps, in the style of the L.-Gds. Finland Regiment [119].

3 May 1817 – The **orange** color prescribed for lower ranks' uniforms, and for officers' shabracks and pistol carriers as well as their uniforms, was ordered to be **changed to red** (Illus. 1974) [120].

8 May 1817 – In order to make the **greatcoats** of the L.-Gds. Jäger Regiment, in the 1st Guards Infantry Division, different from those of the L.-Gds. Finland Regiment in the 2nd Guards Infantry Division, the former was ordered to have greatcoat collars the same as before—dark green with red piping—while the collars of the latter were to add the same red buttonhole loops or patches [*petlitsy ili klapany*] with buttons that were established at this time for the other regiments of the 2nd Guards Infantry Division: Lithuania (later renamed Moscow), Grenadier, and Pavlovsk [121].

12 May 1817 - All combatant ranks in the L.-Gds. Jäger Regiment were ordered to have **coats** with light-green cloth collars, lapels, cuffs, and skirt lining; cuffs were to have red cloth flaps; red piping on the collar and white cloth piping on the lapels, cuffs, cuff flaps, and skirt turnbacksand skirt turnbacks; for officers gold embroidery of a new pattern (Illus. 1975, 1976, and 1977). Thus both regiments of Guards light infantry had lapels that in winter were ordered to be worn closed, except on holidays, and worn open the rest of the time (Illus. 1975 and 1976) [122].

13 May 1817 - In order to relieve the soldier while on campaign and to protect his accouterments, it was laid down that during such times they were always to be in greatcoats and their shako, plume, pouch, and uniform with leggings were to have **covers** [*chekhly*] of raven's-duck or Flemish linen painted with black oil paint in the manner of oilcloth, in all respects according to the instructions laid out above in the description of uniforms for Grenadier regiments [123].

8 August 1817 – The L.-Gds. Jäger Regiment's **forage caps** were ordered to be the same as those of the L.-Gds. Finland Regiment [124].

26 September 1817 - Confirmation was given to a description of **accouterments** and instructions for the manner of wearing them in the Guards light infantry, identical to those issued at this time for Army Carabinier and Jäger regiments, with only the following differences:

a) All metallic items prescribed made of yellow brass [*zheltaya med'*] in Army Carabinier and Jäger regiments were left in the Guards as before—of red brass [copper] (Illus. 1975, 1976, and 1978) [125].

b) On the shako, instead of the small grenade, a two-headed eagle was left as before (Illus. 1975, 1976, and 1978) [126].

c) A badge was issed for the pouch cover, of the same pattern as that established at this time for Carabinier regiments, but of red brass and with the Cyrillic letters L.G.E. in the L.-Gds. Jäger Regiment and L.G.F. in the L.-Gds. Finland Regiment (Illus. 1978) [127].

d) Crossbelts, sword belts, and in general all straps were prescribed to be lacquered and without stiching along the sides, instead of being polished [128].

e) The buckle fastening the knapsack's chest strap was prescribed to be of red brass instead of iron [129].

8 December 1817 - It was ordered that the **leather cuffs on cloth pants** were to have spat-like projections of a pattern similar to the spats on summer pants [130].

2 March 1818 - The newly established **L.-Gds. Volhynia Regiment** in Warsaw as part of the Guards light infantry was prescribed to have the same uniform as the L.-Gds. Finland Regiment, but with yellow piping, white buttons and shako fittings, integral cloth spats instead of leather cuffs; the image of a Lithuanian horseman on the shako plates instead of St. George; badges on pouches with the Cyrillic letters L.G.V.; silver buttonhole loops on officers' coats; shabracks and pistol carriers with yellow piping and silver galloon. A further difference was that round woolen shako pompons were prescribed for Marksmen platoons and Jäger companies in the L.-Gds. Volhynia Regiment: Marksmen Platoon of the 1st Battalion – yellow; of the 2nd Battalion – top half yellow and bottom half green; in the Jäger companies of the 1st Battalion – all white, and in the 2nd Battalion – top half white, bottom half green; for officers – silver (Illus. 1979 and 1980) [131].

4 April 1818 – In the L.-Gds. Jäger Regiment the light-green color for collars, lapels, cuffs, and skirt turnback lining, as well as the corresponding inserts on shabracks and pistol carriers, were all changed to the same **dark-green** color of the coat (Illus. 1981) [132].

23 August 1818 – The length and width of **shoulder straps** on tailcoats and greatcoats was defined, identical to that laid down at this time for Grenadiers and other Army infantry regiments [133], and it was confirmed that musicians' and drummers' coats would have red shoulder wings, the same color as the shoulder strap [134].

23 January 1819 - **Drumsticks** and the **handles of entrenching tools** were ordered to be be black in all Guards light infantry regiments [135].

4 April 1819 - The **spats** on the leggings in use since 1817 were removed [136].

10 April 1819 - The **Hornists** [*Gornisty*] and **Signalers** [*Signalisty*] newly placed on the establishment of Guards light infantry regiments were authorized the same uniform as for drummers, and the **signal horns** [*signalnye rozhki*] were to be of yellow brass, with black straps, and painted inside with green paint, with a gold wreath around the edge (Illus. 1982) [137].

20 September 1820 – Field and company-grade officers of Guards light infantry regiments were given a new pattern **gorget**, identical to that established at this time for the L.-Gds. Izmailovskii, Moscow, Grenadier, and Pavlovsk Regiments [138]. In this same year there was a change in the uniforms of musicians, fifers, signalers, and drummers, consisting of the sewn-on chevrons on their coats beginning to be placed closer together, almost touching one another, and on the swallows' nests the tape was no longer perpendicular as before, but at a diagonal toward the lower edge. Also, all four sides of the collar began to be trimmed with this tape (Illus. 1983) [139].

27 August 1822 – All lower ranks of the L.-Gds. Jäger and Finland Regiments, except the Grenadier platoons, which wore plumes, were ordered to have round **pompons** on the shako: In the Marksmen platoon of the 1st Battalion – yellow (Illus. 1984); of the 2nd Battalion – top half yellow, bottom half green; of the 3rd Battalion – top half yellow, bottom half dark blue; in the Jäger companies of the 1st Battalion – all white; of the 2nd Battalion – top half white, bottom half green; of the 3rd Battalion – top half white, bottom half dark blue (Illus. 1984). Officers were given silver pompons (Illus. 1985) [140].

26 November 1823 - All **musicians** of the named regiments, even though they might not hold non-commissioned officer ranks, were ordered to have: gold galloon on the coat; plumes on the shakos with noncommissioned officers's tops and non-commissioned officers' pompons. This did not apply to hornists, fifers, or drummers who did not hold non-commissioned officer rank [141].

16 January 1824 – The following changes were ordered in the uniforms and accouterments of combatant lower ranks:

1) **Coattails**, which up to this time had one covering the other, were to be cut so that their inner edges came together, and sewn together where they touched (Illus. 1986).

2.) To the decorative end [*trinchik*] of the **shako cords**, which was to be level with the right shoulder, there was to be added a special loop of white cord attached to the button on the right shoulder strap, so that the shako cords stayed in place when the soldier moved about (Illus. 1986).

3.) The **cartridge pouch** was to be worn so that when the soldier bent his elbow, the distance between it and a line with the top edge of the pouch was equal to 3 vershoks [5 1/4 inches].

4.) The **knapsack chest strap** was to be fitted so that it passed between the third and fourth buttons of the coat, as counted from the bottom (Illus. 1986).

5.) On the **musket sling**, opposite the cocking piece, there was to be a band of the same kind of leather as the sling, for stowing the firing cover [*ognivnyi chekhol*] when it needed to be removed (Illus. 1986) [142].

29 March 1825 - For combatant lower ranks, for faultless service, there were established **stripes** [*nashivki*] to be sewn on the left sleeve: for 10 years service - one, for 15 years - two, for 20 years - three; one over the other, all of yellow tape [143].

Soldiers and officer of Guard Regiments

NOTES

(1) *Complete Collection of Laws* [*Polnoe Sobranie Zakonov*, henceforth PSZ], Vol. XXVI, pg. 609, No 19,826.

(2) PSZ Vol. XLIV, Pt. II, regulations for uniforms, page 72, No 19,950.

(3) Ibid., pg. 30, No 20,485, and information received from the War Ministry's Commissariat Department.

(4) Highestconfirmed table of uniforms, accouterments, and weapons for Life-Guards Preobrazhenskii, Semenovskii, and Izmailovskii Regiments, 29 December 1802; drawings of the uniforms of these regiments located in the SOVEREIGN EMPEROR'S Own Library, catalogued under No 54, and actual uniforms and other items preserved up to the present time.

(5) Information received from the War Ministry's Commissariat Department.

(6) Determination made by the Military Collegium, 20 October 1803.

(7) PSZ Vol. XXVIII, pg. 895, No 21,661.

(8) Information received from the War Ministry's Commissariat Department.

(9) Actual officers' hats of that time, preserved up to the present time, and statements by contemporaries.

(10) Information received from the War Ministry's Commissariat Department.

(11) PSZ Vol. XLIV, pg. 31, No 22,197.

(12) From the files of the War Ministry's Commissariat Department.

(13) PSZ Vol. XXIX, pg. 201, No 22,382.

(14) Ibid., Vol. XXIX, pg. 1039, No 22,482.

(15) Information received from the War Ministry's Commissariat Department; uniforms from that time, preserved up to the present, and statements by contemporaries.

(16) PSZ Vol. XLIV, pg. 14, No 22,633, and pg. 13, No 22,720; information received from the War Ministry's Commissariat Department.

(17) Ibid., pg. 13, No 22,727; information received from the War Ministry's Commissariat Dep.,and statements by contemporaries.

(18) Ibid., Vol. XXX, pg. 45, No 22,784, and statements by contemporaries.

(19) Information received from the War Ministry's Commissariat Department.

(20) Files in the Archive of the the War Ministry's Inspection Department, with drawings and descriptions of the manner of wearing knapsacks and greatcoats, 1808, No 13,786/654; information received from the War Ministry's Commissariat Department,and statements from contemporaries.

(21) Information received from the War Ministry's Commissariat Department,and actual gorgets preserved up to now.

(22) PSZ Vol. XLIV, Pt. II, pg. 67, No 23,335.

(23) Ibid., Vol. XXX, pg. 669, No 23,343.

(24) From the files of the War Ministry's Commissariat Department.

(25) PSZ, Vol. XLIV, pg. 13, No 23,548.

(26) From the files of the War Ministry's Commissariat Department.

(27) PSZ, Vol. XXX, pg. 904, No 23,571.

(28) Ibid., pg. 950, No 23,625.

(29) Ibid., pg. 970, No 23,667, and statements from contemporaries.

(30) Ibid., pg. 1006, No 23,695.

(31) Ibid., pg. 1114, No 23,812.

(32) Ibid., pgs. 1364 and 1362 Nos 24,049 and 24,109, HIGHEST Confirmed model shako, 15 December 1809, located in HIS IMPERIAL HIGHNESS's Own Arsenal in the Anichkov Palace, and statements from contemporaries.

(33) Ditto.

(34) From the files of the War Ministry's Commissariat Department.

(35) PSZ Vol. XXXI, pg. 558, No 24,527.

(36) Statements from contemporaries.

(37) PSZ Vol. XXXI, pg. 862, No 24,805.

(38) Ibid., Vol. XLIV, pg. 898, No 24,848.

(39) Ibid., pg. 15, No 24,860, and from the files of the War Ministry's Commissariat Department

(40) From the files of the War Ministry's Commissariat Department, and uniforms from that time, preserved up to now.

(41) The accompanying drawings of embroidery are taken from uniforms of that time.

(42) PSZ Vol. XLIV, pg. 13, No 24,991.

(43) Information received from the L.-Gds. Grenadier Regiment, and contemporary uniform items.

(44) PSZ Vol. XLIV, pg. 104, No 26,992.

(45) From the files of the War Ministry's Commissariat Department.

(46) PSZ Vol. XXXIII, pg. 23, No 25,782.

(47) See below, entry for 11 February 1815.

(48) From the files of the War Ministry's Commissariat Department, and statements from contemporaries.

(49) PSZ Vol. XXXIII, pg. 23, No 25,782.

(50) Ibid., pg. 450, No 26,095, and from the files of the War Ministry's Commissariat Department.

(51) Ibid., Vol. XLIV, pg. 104, No 26,842.

(52) HIGHEST Confirmed, 12 May 1817, description of the uniforms of the regiments of the 1st Guards Infantry Division, and model uniforms preserved in the War Ministry's Commissariat Department.

(53) PSZ Vol. XLIV, pg. 120.

(54) Ibid., pg. 104, No 26,992.

(55) Ibid., pgs. 104-108, No 27,067.

(56) Ibid.

(57) Ibid.

(58) Ibid.

(59) Ibid.

(60) From the files of the War Ministry's Commissariat Department.

(61) PSZ Vol. XLIV, pg. 103, No 27,298; model uniforms preserved at the War Ministry's Commissariat Department, and officers' uniforms and other items from that time.

(62) PSZ Vol. XLIV, pg. 121, No 27,504.

(63) Ibid., pg. 122.

(64) Ibid., pg. 108, No 27,653.

(65) Order of the Chief of H.I.M. Main Staff, 4 April 1819, No 21.

(66) From the files of the War Ministry's Commissariat Department; signal horns of that time preserved up to now, and contemporary drawings.

(67) From the files of the War Ministry's Commissariat Department.

(68) PSZ Vol. XLIV, pg. 122, No 29,658.

(69) Order to the Separate Corps of Military Settlements, 16 January 1824, No 22, and contemporary drawings and uniforms.

(70) PSZ Vol. XL, pg. 188, No 30,309.

(71) Information received from the Chancellery of the L.-Gds. Pavlovsk Regiment.

(72) PSZ Vol. XXVI, pg. 609, No 19,826.

(73) Ibid., Vol. XLIV, pg. 71, No 19,874.

(74) Ibid., Vol. XIV, pg. 72, No 19,950.

(75) Ibid., pg. 30, No 20,485, and from the files of the War Ministry's Commissariat Department.

(76) Announcement by the Government Military Collegium to the Military Commission, 16 September 1802, and drawings held in the SOVEREIGN EMPEROR's Own Library, catalogued as No 54.

(77) HighestConfirmed table of uniforms, accouterments, and weapons for the L.-Gds. Jäger Battalion, 29 December 1802; drawings of uniforms of this battalion, located in the SOVEREIGN EMPEROR's Own Library, catalogued as No 54, and actual uniforms and other items preserved up to the present time.

(78) From the files of the War Ministry's Commissariat Department.

(79) PSZ Vol. XLIV, pg. 71, No 21,117; contemporary drawings and statements from contemporaries.

(80) Determination made by the Government Military Collegium, 4 August 1804, and statements from contemporaries.

(81) From the files of the War Ministry's Commissariat Department.

(82) Ditto.

(83) PSZ Vol. XXIV, pg. 789, No 22,321, and a model front pouch preserved at the War Ministry's Commissariat Department.

(84) Ibid., pg. 201, No 22,382.

(85) From the files of the War Ministry's Commissariat Department.

(86) Statements from contemporaries.

(87) PSZ Vol. XLIV, pg. 14, No 22,633.

(88) Ibid., Vol. XLIV, pg. 54, No 22,727, and statements from contemporaries.

(89) PSZ Vol. XLIV, pg. 13, No 22,720, and statements from contemporaries.

(90) Ibid., pg. 13, No 22,727; from the files of the War Ministry's Commissariat Department, and statements from contemporaries.

(91) Ibid., Vol. XXX, pg. 45, No 22,784, and statements from contemporaries.

(92) From the files of the War Ministry's Commissariat Department.

(93) PSZ Vol. XLIV, pg. 15, No 22,965; drawings of uniforms of the IMPERIAL Militia Battalion located in HIS IMPERIAL HIGHNESS GRAND DUKE MICHAEL PAVLOVICH'S Own Library, and HighestConfirmed table of uniforms, accouterments, and arms of the L.-Gds. Finland Battalion, 21 January 1809.

(94) Statements from contemporaries.

(95) PSZ Vol. XXX, pg. 128, No 22,895; ibid., Vol. XLIV, pg. 67, No 23,335, and statements from contemporaries.

(96) File in the Archives of the War Ministsry's Inspection Department, with drawings and descriptions of how to wear knapsacks and greatcoats, No 13,786-654; from the files of the War Ministry's Commissariat Department, and and statements from contemporaries.

(97) PSZ Vol. XLIV, Pt. II, pg. 67, No 23,335.

(98) Ibid., Vol. XXX, pg. 669, No 23,343.

(99) HighestConfirmed table of uniforms, accouterments, and weapons for the L.-Gds. Finland Regiment, 21 January 1809.

(100) From the files of the War Ministry's Commissariat Department.

(101) PSZ, Vol. XXX, pg. 904, No 23,571, and pg. 950, No 23,625.

(102) Ibid., Vol. XXX, pg. 965, No 23,654.
(103) Ibid., pg. 1006, No 23,695.
(104) Ibid., pgs. 1362 No 24,019, and pg. 1364, No 24,049.
(105) HIGHEST Confirmed model shako, 15 December 1809, located in HIS IMPERIAL HIGHNESS's Own Arsenal in the Anichkov Palace, and statements from contemporaries.
(106) From the files of the War Ministry's Commissariat Department.
(107) Ditto.
(108) PSZ Vol. XXXI, pg. 557, No 24,526, and pg. 558, No 24,527, and from the files of the War Ministry's Commissariat Department.
(109) Statements from contemporaries.
(110) From the files of the War Ministry's Commissariat Department.
(111) Statements from contemporaries.
(112) PSZ Vol. XXXI, pg. 898, No 24,848.
(113) From the files of the War Ministry's Commissariat Department, and uniforms from that time, preserved up to the present time.
(114) Embroidery on uniform coats from that time.
(115) PSZ Vol. XLIV, pg. 13, No 24,991.
(116) From the files of the War Ministry's Commissariat Department, and statements from contemporaries
(117) Ditto.
(118) PSZ Vol. XXXIII, pg. 450 , No 26,095, and from the files of the War Ministry's Commissariat Department
(119) PSZ Vol. XLIV, pg. 103, No 26,655.
(120) From the files of the War Ministry's Commissariat Department.
(121) PSZ Vol. XLIV, pg. 104, No 26,842.
(122) HIGHEST Confirmed, 12 May 1817, description of the uniforms of the regiments of the 1st Guards Infantry Division, and model uniforms preserved in the War Ministry's Commissariat Department.
(123) PSZ Vol. XLIV, pg. 120.
(124) Ibid., pg. 104, No 26,992.
(125) Ibid., pgs. 104-108, No 27,067.
(126) Ditto.
(127) Ditto.
(128) Ditto.
(129) Ditto.
(130) From the files of the War Ministry's Commissariat Department.
(131) PSZ Vol. XLIV, pg. 103, No 27,298; model uniforms preserved at the War Ministry's Commissariat Department, and officers' uniforms and other items from that time.
(132) Memorandum by War Ministry's Commissariat Department to the Commission of the St.-Petersburg Commissariat Depot, 4 April 1818, and HIGHESTConfirmed model uniform clothing preserved at the War Ministy's Commissariat Department.
(133) PSZ Vol. XLIV, pg. 121, No 27,504.
(134) Ibid., pg. 122.
(135) Ibid., pg. 108, No 27,653.
(136) Order of the Chief of H.I.M. Main Staff, 4 April 1819, No 21.
(137) From the files of the War Ministry's Commissariat Department; signal horns of that time preserved up to now, and contemporary drawings.
(138) From the files of the War Ministry's Commissariat Department.
(139) Ditto.
(140) PSZ Vol. XLV, pg. 103, No 19,171, and statements from contemporaries.
(141) PSZ Vol. XLIV, pg. 122, No 29,658.
(142) Order to the Separate Corps of Military Settlements, 16 January 1824, No 22, and contemporary drawings and uniforms.
(143) PSZ Vol. XL, pg. 188, No 30,309.

Soldiers and officer of Guard Infantry Regiment

РИСУНКИ
ОДЕЖДЫ и ВООРУЖЕНІЯ
РОССІЙСКИХЪ
ВОЙСКЪ
1801-1825.

PLATES LIST OF ILLUSTRATIONS

1910. Officers' coat embroidery for the L.-Gds. Izmailovskii Regiment, since 1812.

1911. Officers' coat embroidery for the L.-Gds. Lithuania Regiment (now the L.-Gds. Moscow Reg.), since 1812.

1912. Private Non-Combatants. -1806. L.-Gds Preobrazhenskii and Semenovskii Regiments, 1812-1817.

1913. Non-Combatants holding NCO rank. L.-Gds. Izmailovskii and Lithuania Regiments, 1812-1817.

1914. Company-grade Officer and Private. L.-Gds. Grenadier Regiment, 1813-1816.

1915. Private and Field-Grade Officer. L.-Gds. Pavlovsk Regiment, 1813-1816.

1916. Drum-Major epaulettes, staves, and pompons, established in 1815. a. Regiments of the Old Guard. b) Regiments of the Young Guard.

1917. Drum Majors. L.-Gds. Preobrazhenskii and L.-Gds. Grenadier Regiments, 1815-1816.

1918. Shabracks and pistol carriers of the L.-Gds. Grenadier and Pavlovsk Regiments, established 11 Feb. 1815.

1919. Privates. L.-Gds. Moscow, Grenadier, and Pavlovsk Regiments, 1817-1825.

1920. Grenadier. L.-Gds. Preobrazhenskii Regiment, 1817-1825. Note. In 1824, for the entire Guards infantry, a loop was attached to the button on the right shoulder strap, as shown below in Illus. 1611.

1921. Adjutant. L.-Gds. Preobrazhenskii Regiment, 1817-1825.

1922. Non-commissioned Officer. L.-Gds. Semenovskii Regiment, 1817-1825.

1923. Company-Grade Officers. L.-Gds. Semenovskii Regiment, 1817-1825.

1924. Field-Grade Officer. L.-Gd. Izmailovskii Regiment, 1817-1825.

1925. Private and Company-Grade Officer. L.-Gd. Moscow Regiment, 1817-1825.

1926. Field-Grade Officer and Grenadiers. . L.-Gd. Grenadier Regiment, 1817-1825.

1927. Field-Grade Officer and Drummer. . L.-Gd. Pavlovsk Regiment, 1817-1818.

1928. Private. L.-Gds. Lithuania Regiment, 1817-1825.

1929. Guards shako badge, with the image of a Lithuanian horseman, instituted in 1818.

1930. Hornist. L.-Gds. Semenovskii Regiment, 1820-1825.

1931. Company-Grade Officer. L.-Gds. Lithuania Regiment, 1818-1820.

1932. Field-Grade Officers. L.-Gds. Lithuania Regiment, 1818-1820.

1933. Drum Major and Musician. L.-Gds. Izmailovskii Regiment, 1818-1820.

1934. Musician. L.-Gds. Lithuania Regiment, 1818-1820.

1935. Drummers. L.-Gds. Grenadier and Pavlovsk Regiments, 1818-1820.

1936. Signaler and Drummer. L.-Gds. Preobrazhenskii Regiment, 1819-1820.

1937. Guards officers' gorgets, instituted 20 September 1820. a. Ensign, b. Sublieutenant, c. Lieutenant, d. Staff-Captain, e. Captain, f. Field-grade officers. Note: the inscription "1700. No. 19." was awarded as a distinction to only to the Preobrazhenskii and Semenovskii regiments.

1938. Non-Commissioned Officer. L.-Gds. Lithuania Regiment, 1818-1825.

1939. Grenadiers. L.-Gds. Semenovskii and L.-Gds. Izmailovskii Regiments, 1824-1825.

1939a. Officer's headdress in the L.-Gds. Pavlovsk Regiment, established in May 1825.

1940. Private and Non-Commissioned Officer. L.-Gds. Jäger Battalion, 1802-1804.

1941. Company Drummer. L.-Gds. Jäger Battalion, 1802-1804.

1942. Battalion Drummer and Waldhornist. L.-Gds. Jäger Battalion, 1802-1804.

1943. Field and Company-Grade Officers. L.-Gds. Jäger Battalion, 1802-1804.

1944. General and Clerk. L.-Gds. Jäger Battalion, 1802-1804.

1945. Shabrack and pistol carrier for the L.-Gds. Jäger Regiment, 1804-1810.

1946. Company-Grade Officer. L.-Gds. Jäger Battalion, 1804-1806.

1947. Private and Non-Commissioned Officer. L.-Gds. Jäger Battalion, 1804-1806.

1948. Battalion Drummer. L.-Gds. Jäger Battalion, 1804-1806.

1949. Private. L.-Gds. Jäger Battalion. 1806-1807.

1950. Company-Grade Officer. L.-Gds. Jäger Battalion, 1807-1808.

1951. Privates. L.-Gds. Jäger Regiment, 1808-1809.

1952. Non-Commissioned Officer. L.-Gds. Jäger Regiment, 1808.

1953. Company-Grade Officers. L.-Gds. Jäger Regiment, 1808-1809.

1954. Grenadiers. L.-Gds. Finland Battalion, 1808-1810.

1955. Jägers. L.-Gds. Finland Battalion, 1808-1810.

1956. Grenadier Non-Commissioned Officer and Jäger Drummer. L.-Gds. Jäger Regiment, 1808-1810.

1957. Company-Grade Officers. Grenadier and Jäger Companies of the L.-Gds. Jäger Regiment, 1808-1810.

1958. Shabrack and pistol carriers of the L.-Gds. Finland Battalion, established in 1808.

1959. Private. L.-Gds. Jäger Regiment, 1810.

1960. Craftsman and Clerk. L.-Gds. Finland Battalion, 1809-1811.

1961. Non-Commissioned Officers. L.-Gds. Jäger Regiment and Finland Battalion, 1808-1810.

1962. Company-Grade Officers. L.-Gds. Jäger Regiment and Finland Battalion, 1809-1810.

1963. Company Drummer, L.-Gds. Jäger Regiment. NCO, L.-Gds. Finland Battalion. 1810-1811.

1964. Shabrack and pistol carriers of the L.-Gds. Jäger Regiment, 1810-1817.

1965. Grenadiers. L.-Gds. Jäger Regiment and L.-Gds. Finland Battalion, 1811.

1966. Grenadier Non-Commissioned Officer. L.-Gds. Jäger Regiment, 1811.

1967. Grenadier Company-Grade Officers. L.-Gds. Jäger Regiment and L.-Gds. Finland Battalion, 1811.

1968. Forage caps of the L.-Gds. Jäger and Finland Regiments, established in 1811.

1969. Field-Grade Officer and Jäger. L.-Gds. Jäger Regiment, 1812-1816.

1970. Private and Company-Grade Officer. Grenadier Companies of the L.-Gds. Jäger Regiment, 1812-1814.

1971. Grenadier, Jäger, and Drummer. L.-Gds. Finland Regiment, 1812-1816.

1972. Field-Grade Officer and Grenadier Company-Grade Officer. L.-Gds. Finland Regiment, 1812-1816.

1973. NCO Privates. L.-Gds. Jäger and Finland Regiments, 1812-1825.

1974. Field-Grade Officer and Private. L.-Gds. Jäger Regiment, 1817.

1975. Marksman. L.-Gds. Jäger Regiment, 1817-1818.

1976. Company-Grade Officers. L.-Gds. Jäger Regiment, 1817-1818.

1977. Officers' embroidery on coats in the L.-Gds. Jäger Regiment, from 1817.

1978. Carabinier and Jäger. L.-Gds. Finland Regiment, 1817-1822.

1979. Marksman. L.-Gds. Volhynia Regiment, 1818-1825.

1980. Field-Grade Officer. L.-Gds. Volhynia Regiment, 1817-1820.

1981. Field-Grade Officer and Private. L.-Gds. Jäger Regiment, 1818-1822.

1982. Hornist. L.-Gds. Jäger Regiment, 1819-1820.

1983. Fifer. L.-Gds. Finland Regiment, 1820-1825.

1984. Non-Commissioned Officers. L.-Gds. Jäger and Finland Regiments, 1822-1823.

1985. Company-Grade Officers. L.-Gds. Jäger and Finland Regiments, 1822-1825.

1986. Privates. L.-Gds. Jäger, Finland, and Volhynia Regiments, 1824-1825.

Privates. L.Gds Preobrazhenskii, Semenovskii, and Izmailovskii Regiments, 1802-1805

Guards Helmets, 1802-1805. (Private and Non-Commissioned Officer)

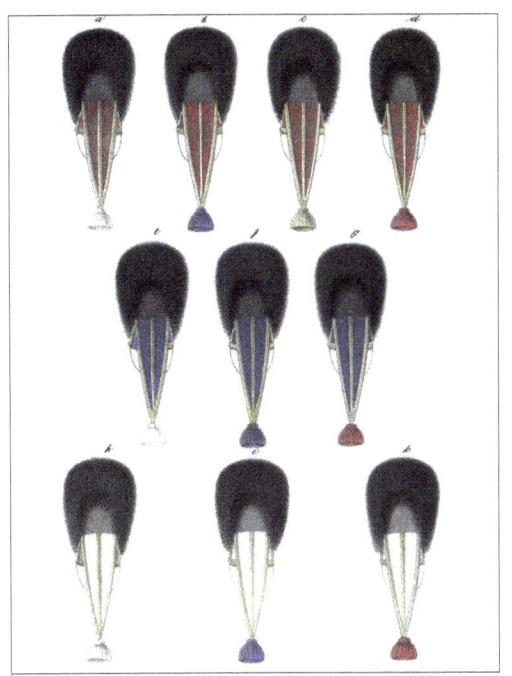

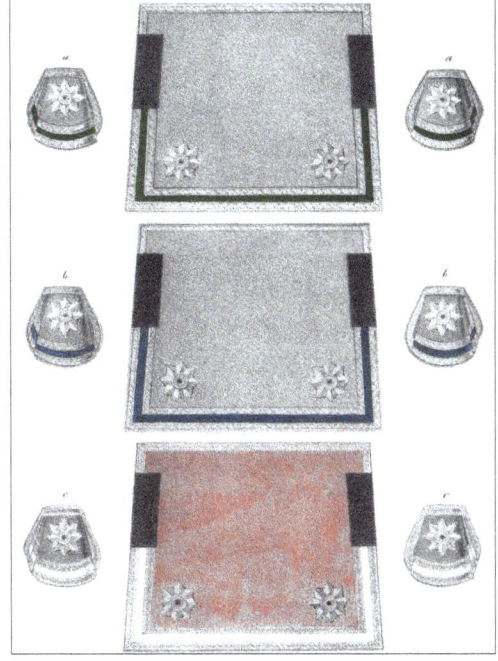

Guards Helmets, 1802-1805 - Guards Officers' Shabracks and Pistol Carriers, established in 1804 - Guards Shako Badge, established 16 April 1808

Non-Commissioned Officers. L.-Gds. Preobrazhenskii Regiment, 1802-1805

Non-Commissioned Officers. L.-Gds. Izmailovskii Regiment, 1802-1805

Non-Commissioned Officer. L.-Gds Izmailovskii Regiment, 1802-1805

Company Drummer. L.-Gds Preobrazhenskii Regiment, 1802-1805

Fifer. L.-Gds. Semenovskii Regiment, 1802-1805

Company Drummer and Musician. L.-Gds Izmailovskii Regiment, 1802-1805

Company-Grade Officers. L.-Gds Preobrazhenskii Regiment, 1802-1807

Field-Grade Officer. L.-Gds. Semenovskii Regiment, 1802-1807

General. L.-Gds Izmailovskii Regiment, 1802-1807

Private and Non-Commissioned Officer. L.-Gds Preobrazhenskii Regiment, 1804-1807

Company Drummer and Fifer. L.-Gds. Semenovskii Regiment, 1804-1807

Musician. L.-Gds Izmailovskii Regiment, 1804-1807

Company-Grade Officer. L.-Gds. Preobrazhenskii Regiment, 1808

Privates. L.-Gds. Semenovskii Regiment, 1808

Guards Shako, 1808-1810

Guards Non-Commissioned Officer's Shako, 1808-1810

Guards Officer's Shako, 1808-1809

Privates. L.-Gds Izmailovskii Regiment, 1808-1809

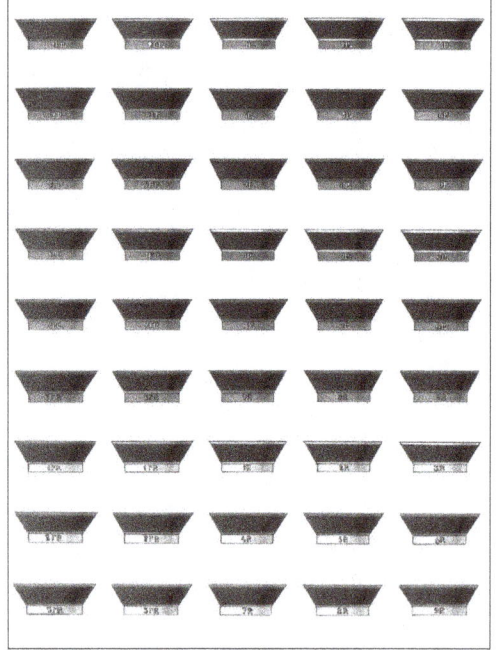

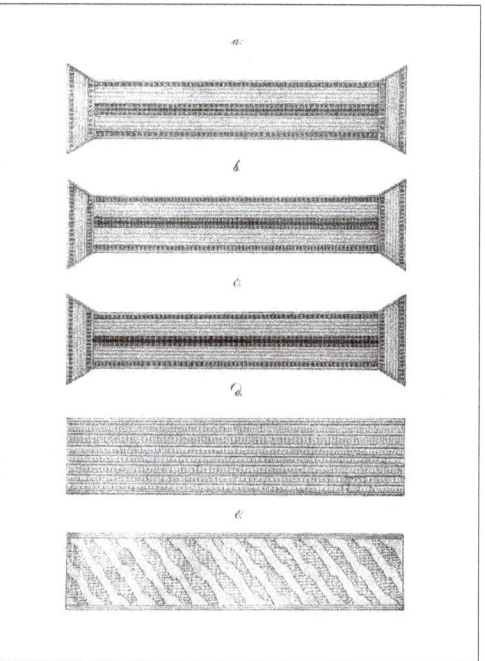

Badge on Guards pouches, established in 1808 - Guards Officers' gorgets, established 20 June 1808 - Forage caps for lower ranks of the L.-Gds

Company-grade Officer and Sergeant. L.-Gds. Preobrazhenskii Regiment 1809-1810

Company-grade Officers. L-Gds. Semenovskii Regiment, 1810

Private and Musician. L.-Gds Izmailovskii Regiment, 1810-1811

Field-Grade Officer and Drummer. L.-Gds. Lithuania Regiment, 1811

Company-grade Officer and Non-Commissioned Officer. L.-Gds. Preobrazhenskii Regiment, 1812-1816

Company-grade Officer. L-Gds. Semenovskii Regiment, 1812-1816

Private. L-Gds. Semenovskii Regiment, 1812-1816

Company-grade Officer and Lower Ranks. L.-Gds Izmailovskii Regiment, 1812-1816

Private and Adjutant. L.-Gds. Lithuania Regiment, 1812-1816

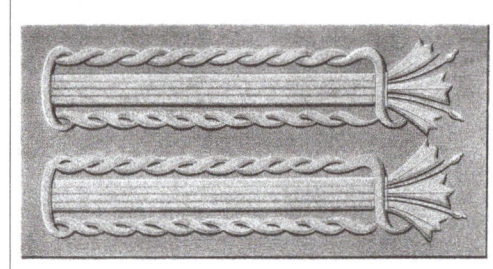

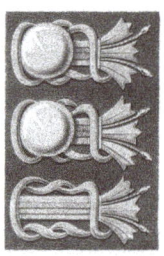

Officers' coat embroidery for the L.-Gds. Preobrazhenskii, Semenovskii, Izmailovskii   Regiment and Lithuania Regiment (now the L.-Gds. Moscow Regiment), since 1812

Private NCO. 1806. L.-Gds Preobrazhenskii and Semenovskii Regiments, 1812-1817

NCO holding non-commissioned officer rank. L.-Gds. Izmailovskii and Lithuania Regiments, 1812-1817

Company-grade Officer and Private. L.-Gds. Grenadier Regiment, 1813-1816

Private and Field-Grade Officer. L.-Gds. Pavlovsk Regiment, 1813-1816

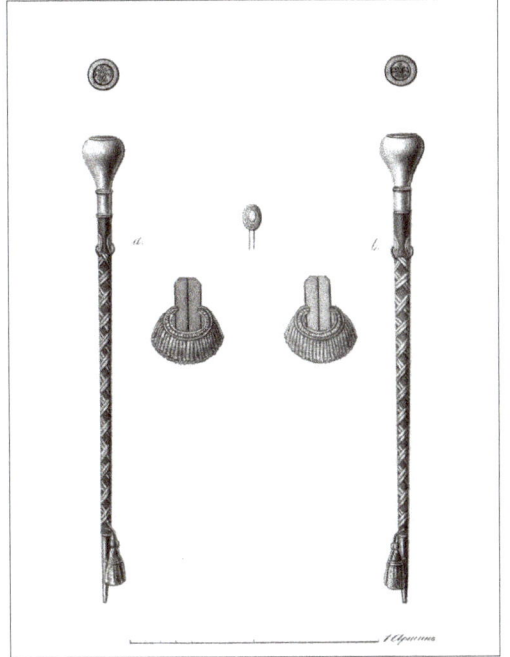

Drum-Major epaulettes, staves, and pompons, established in 1815 - Shabracks and pistol carriers of the L.-Gds. Grenadier and Pavlovsk Regiments, established 11 February 1815 - Guards shako badge, with the image of a Lithuanian horseman, instituted in 1818

Drum Majors. L.-Gds. Preobrazhenskii and L.-Gds. Grenadier Regiments, 1815-1816

Privates. L.-Gds. Moscow, Grenadier, and Pavlovsk Regiments, 1817-1825

Grenadier. L.-Gds. Preobrazhenskii Regiment, 1817-1825

Adjutant. L.-Gds. Preobrazhenskii Regiment, 1817-1825

Non-commissioned Officer. L.-Gds. Semenovskii Regiment, 1817-1825

Company-Grade Officers. L.-Gds. Semenovskii Regiment, 1817-1825

Field-Grade Officer. L.-Gd. Izmailovskii Regiment, 1817-1825

Private and Company-Grade Officer. L.-Gd. Moscow Regiment, 1817-1825

Field-Grade Officer and Grenadiers. L.-Gd. Grenadier Regiment, 1817-1825

Field-Grade Officer and Drummer. L.-Gd. Pavlovsk Regiment, 1817-1818

Private. L.-Gds. Lithuania Regiment, 1817-1825

Hornist. L.-Gds. Semenovskii Regiment, 1820-1825

Company-Grade Officer. L.-Gds. Lithuania Regiment, 1818-1820

Field-Grade Officers. L.-Gds. Lithuania Regiment, 1818-1820

Drum Major and Musician. L.-Gds. Izmailovskii Regiment, 1818-1820

Musician. L.-Gds. Lithuania Regiment, 1818-1820

Drummers. L.-Gds. Grenadier and Pavlovsk Regiments, 1818-1820

Signaler and Drummer. L.-Gds. Preobrazhenskii Regiment, 1819-1820

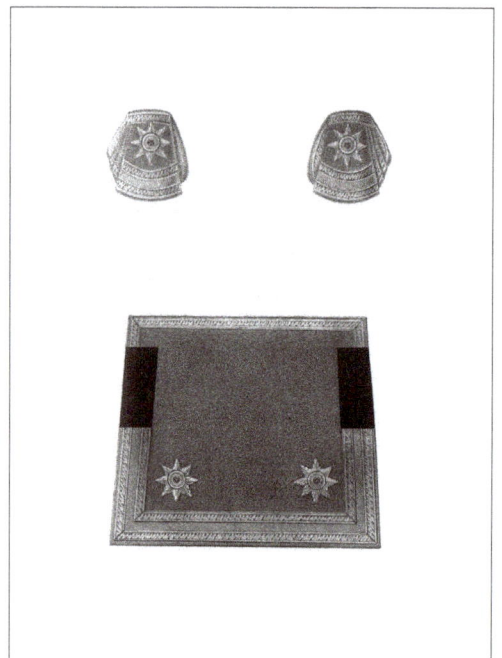

Guards officers' gorgets, instituted 20 September 1820 - Shabrack and pistol carrier for the L.-Gds. Jäger Regiment, 1804-1810, Finland Battalion, established in 1808 and Jäger Regiment, 1810-1817

Non-Commissioned Officer. L.-Gds. Lithuania Regiment, 1818-1825

Grenadiers. L.-Gds. Semenovskii and L.-Gds. Izmailovskii Regiments, 1824-1825

Officer's headdress in the L.-Gds. Pavlovsk Regiment, established in May 1825

Private and Non-Commissioned Officer. L.-Gds. Jäger Battalion, 1802-1804

Company Drummer. L.-Gds. Jäger Battalion, 1802-1804

Battalion Drummer and Waldhornist. L.-Gds. Jäger Battalion, 1802-1804

Field and Company-Grade Officers. L.-Gds. Jäger Battalion, 1802-1804

General and Clerk. L.-Gds. Jäger Battalion, 1802-1804

Company-Grade Officer. L.-Gds. Jäger Battalion, 1804-1806

Private and Non-Commissioned Officer. L.-Gds. Jäger Battalion, 1804-1806

Battalion Drummer. L.-Gds. Jäger Battalion, 1804-1806

Private. L.-Gds. Jäger Battalion. 1806-1807

Company-Grade Officer. L.-Gds. Jäger Battalion, 1807-1808

Privates. L.-Gds. Jäger Regiment, 1808-1809

Non-Commissioned Officer. L.-Gds. Jäger Regiment, 1808

Company-Grade Officers. L.-Gds. Jäger Regiment, 1808-1809

Grenadiers. L.-Gds. Finland Battalion, 1808-1810

Jägers. L.-Gds. Finland Battalion, 1808-1810

Grenadier Non-Commissioned Officer and Jäger Drummer. L.-Gds. Jäger Regiment, 1808-1810

Company-Grade Officers. Grenadier and Jäger Companies of the L.-Gds. Jäger Regiment, 1808-1810

Private. L.-Gds. Jäger Regiment, 1810

Craftsman and Clerk. L.-Gds. Finland Battalion, 1809-1811

Non-Commissioned Officers. L.-Gds. Jäger Regiment and Finland Battalion, 1808-1810

Company-Grade Officers. L.-Gds. Jäger Regiment and Finland Battalion, 1809-1810

Company Drummer, L.-Gds. Jäger Regiment. Non-Commissioned Officer, L.-Gds. Finland Battalion. 1810-1811

Grenadiers. L.-Gds. Jäger Regiment and L.-Gds. Finland Battalion, 1811

Grenadier Non-Commissioned Officer. L.-Gds. Jäger Regiment, 1811

Grenadier Company-Grade Officers. L.-Gds. Jäger Regiment and L.-Gds. Finland Battalion, 1811

Forage caps of the L.-Gds. Jäger and Finland Regiments, established in 1811

Field-Grade Officer and Jäger. L.-Gds. Jäger Regiment, 1812-1816

Private and Company-Grade Officer. Grenadier Companies of the L.-Gds. Jäger Regiment, 1812-1814

Grenadier, Jäger, and Drummer. L.-Gds. Finland Regiment, 1812-1816

Field-Grade Officer and Grenadier Company-Grade Officer. L.-Gds. Finland Regiment, 1812-1816

NCO Privates. L.-Gds Jäger and Finland Regiments, 1812-1825

Field-Grade Officer and Private. L.-Gds Jäger Regiment, 1817

Marksman. L.-Gds. Jäger Regiment, 1817-1818

Company-Grade Officers. L.-Gds. Jäger Regiment, 1817-1818

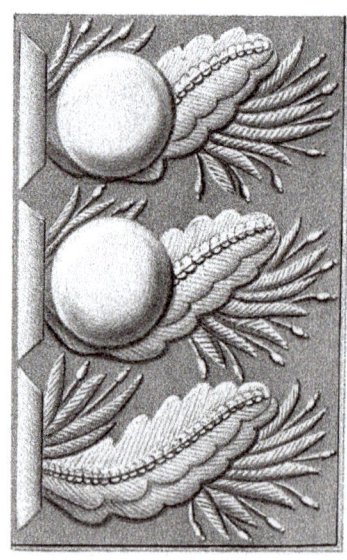

Officers' embroidery on coats in the L.-Gds. Jäger Regiment, from 1817

Carabinier and Jäger. L.-Gds. Finland Regiment, 1817-1822.

Marksman. L.-Gds. Volhynia Regiment, 1818-1825

Field-Grade Officer. L.-Gds. Volhynia Regiment, 1817-1820

Field-Grade Officer and Private. L.-Gds. Jäger Regiment, 1818-1822

Hornist. L.-Gds. Jäger Regiment, 1819-1820

Fifer. L.-Gds. Finland Regiment, 1820-1825

Non-Commissioned Officers. L.-Gds. Jäger and Finland Regiments, 1822-1823

Company-Grade Officers. L.-Gds. Jäger and Finland Regiments, 1822-1825

Privates. L.-Gds. Jäger, Finland, and Volhynia Regiments, 1824-1825

SOLDIERS, WEAPONS & UNIFORMS ALREADY PUBLISHED
(SOME TITLES)

UNIFORMS OF RUSSIAN ARMY IN THE ERA OF ANCIENT TZAR
FROM THE REIGN OF VASILI IV TO MICHAEL I, ALEXIS, FEODOR III DURING THE XVII th CENTURY
A.V.VISKOVATOV — LUCA STEFANO CRISTINI
SWU-600-004

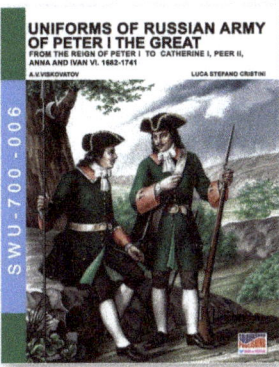

UNIFORMS OF RUSSIAN ARMY OF PETER I THE GREAT
FROM THE REIGN OF PETER I TO CATHERINE I, PEER II, ANNA AND IVAN VI. 1682-1741
A.V.VISKOVATOV — LUCA STEFANO CRISTINI
SWU-700-006

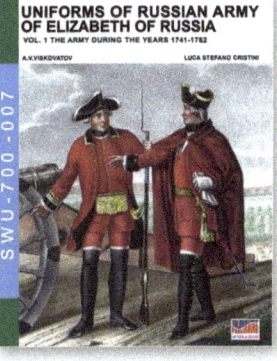

UNIFORMS OF RUSSIAN ARMY OF ELIZABETH OF RUSSIA
VOL. 1 THE ARMY DURING THE YEARS 1741-1762
A.V.VISKOVATOV — LUCA STEFANO CRISTINI
SWU-700-007

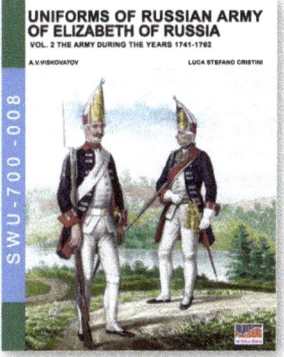

UNIFORMS OF RUSSIAN ARMY OF ELIZABETH OF RUSSIA
VOL. 2 THE ARMY DURING THE YEARS 1741-1762
A.V.VISKOVATOV — LUCA STEFANO CRISTINI
SWU-700-008

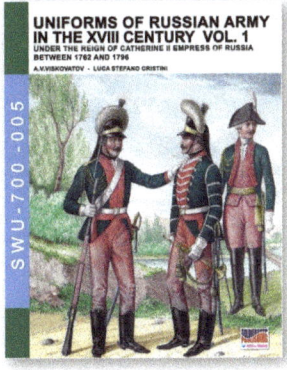

UNIFORMS OF RUSSIAN ARMY IN THE XVIII CENTURY VOL. 1
UNDER THE REIGN OF CATHERINE II EMPRESS OF RUSSIA BETWEEN 1762 AND 1796
A.V.VISKOVATOV — LUCA STEFANO CRISTINI
SWU-700-005

UNIFORMS OF RUSSIAN ARMY IN THE XVIII CENTURY VOL. 2
UNDER THE REIGN OF CATHERINE II EMPRESS OF RUSSIA BETWEEN 1762 AND 1796
A.V.VISKOVATOV — LUCA STEFANO CRISTINI
SWU-700-009

UNIFORMS OF RUSSIAN ARMY IN THE XVIII CENTURY VOL. 3
UNDER THE REIGN OF CATHERINE II EMPRESS OF RUSSIA BETWEEN 1762 AND 1796
A.V.VISKOVATOV — LUCA STEFANO CRISTINI
SWU-700-010

UNIFORMS OF RUSSIAN ARMY IN THE XVIII CENTURY VOL. 4
UNDER THE REIGN OF CATHERINE II EMPRESS OF RUSSIA BETWEEN 1762 AND 1796
A.V.VISKOVATOV — LUCA STEFANO CRISTINI
SWU-700-011

BRITISH ARMY UNIFORMS IN 1742
IN THE ART OF JOHN PINE
SWU-700-001

PRUSSIAN & AUSTRIAN ARMY UNIFORMS IN 1742-1770
LUCA STEFANO CRISTINI
SWU-700-002

THE FRENCH ARMY OF ANCIEN RÉGIME Volume 1
IN THE ART OF FELIX PHILIPPOTEAUX
LUCA STEFANO CRISTINI
SWU-700-003

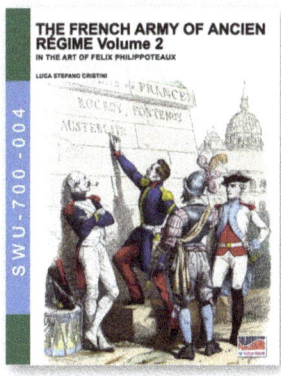

THE FRENCH ARMY OF ANCIEN RÉGIME Volume 2
IN THE ART OF FELIX PHILIPPOTEAUX
LUCA STEFANO CRISTINI
SWU-700-004

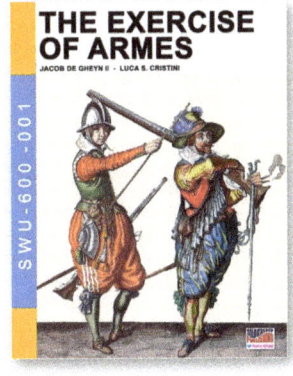

THE EXERCISE OF ARMES
JACOB DE GHEYN — LUCA S. CRISTINI
SWU-600-001

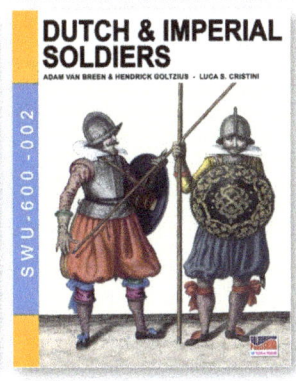

DUTCH & IMPERIAL SOLDIERS
ADAM VAN BREEN & HENDRICK GOLTZIUS — LUCA S. CRISTINI
SWU-600-002

HORSEMEN IN THE 16TH & 17TH C.
JACOB DE GHEYN II — A.DE BRUYN - LUCA S. CRISTINI
SWU-600-003

IMPERIAL SOLDIERS & UNIFORMS 1640-1860
IN THE ART OF FRANZ GERASCH
LUCA S.CRISTINI
Plates by FRANZ GERASCH
SWU-GEN-001

www.ingramcontent.com/pod-product-compliance
Lightning Source LLC
Chambersburg PA
CBHW041142120626
46547CB00020B/3083